Additional Praise for
The Little Book of Bulletproof Investing

"Leave it to my media pal Ben Stein to put me and the media in perspective. We can scare you. That doesn't mean you should let us. Both Ben and Phil DeMuth offer some timely investment tips on how you can make damn sure we don't!"

Neil Cavuto, Senior Vice President and Anchor
Fox News, Fox Business News

THE LITTLE BOOK
OF
BULLETPROOF
INVESTING

Little Book Big Profits Series

In the *Little Book Big Profits* series, the brightest icons in the financial world write on topics that range from tried-and-true investment strategies to tomorrow's new trends. Each book offers a unique perspective on investing, allowing the reader to pick and choose from the very best in investment advice today.

Books in the *Little Book Big Profits* series include:

The Little Book That Beats the Market by Joel Greenblatt
The Little Book of Value Investing by Christopher Browne
The Little Book of Common Sense Investing by John C. Bogle
The Little Book That Makes You Rich by Louis Navellier
The Little Book That Builds Wealth by Pat Dorsey
The Little Book That Saves Your Assets by David M. Darst
The Little Book of Bull Moves in Bear Markets by Peter D. Schiff
The Little Book of Main Street Money by Jonathan Clements
The Little Book of Safe Money by Jason Zweig
The Little Book of Behavioral Investing by James Montier
The Little Book of Big Dividends by Charles B. Carlson
The Little Book of Bulletproof Investing by Ben Stein and Phil DeMuth

THE LITTLE BOOK

OF
BULLETPROOF
INVESTING

Do's and Don'ts to Protect Your

Financial Life

BEN STEIN
PHIL DEMUTH

WILEY

John Wiley & Sons, Inc.

Published by John Wiley & Sons, Inc., Hoboken, New Jersey.
Published simultaneously in Canada.

For general information on our other products and services or for technical support, please contact our Customer Care Department within the United States at (800) 762-2974, outside the United States at (317) 572-3993 or fax (317) 572-4002.

Wiley also publishes its books in a variety of electronic formats. Some content that appears in print may not be available in electronic books. For more information about Wiley products, visit our web site at www.wiley.com.

Library of Congress Cataloging-in-Publication Data

Stein, Benjamin, 1944-
    The little book of bulletproof investing : do's and don'ts to protect your financial life / Ben Stein, Phil DeMuth.
        p.   cm.—(Little book, big profits series)
    Includes index.
    ISBN 978-0-470-56805-7 (cloth)
        1. Investments.   2. Finance, Personal.   I. DeMuth, Phil, 1950-   II. Title.   III. Series.
HG4521.S7553 2010
332.67'8—dc22

                                                                                                            2009054385

Printed in the United States of America
10 9 8 7 6 5 4 3 2 1

For Alex and Julia

Contents

Introduction: Check In with the Control Tower   1

Chapter One
The Nut Behind the Wheel: Behavioral
     Finance in One Lesson   11

Chapter Two
Wall Street Therapy: For Good and for Evil   23

Chapter Three
How Not to Invest: Kids, Don't Try
     This at Home   39

Chapter Four
How to Invest: It's Not as Fun as
     It Used to Be   53

Chapter Five
The Holy Grail of Investing: Having Your
   Cake and Eating It, Too   67

Chapter Six
Bulletproofing Your Investments: A Recipe
   for Setting Up Your Tangent Portfolios   83

Chapter Seven
Pulling the Trigger: Practicing Portfolio
   Management at Home for Fun
   and Profit   95

Chapter Eight
Become the CEO of You, Inc.: Get Wise,
   Get Smart, Get (Further) Educated   107

Chapter Nine
Human Capital 411: Your Personal Human
   Potential Movement   119

Chapter Ten
Save 'Til You Drop: Topping off Your
   Piggy Bank   135

Chapter Eleven
Houses of Blues: Welcome to the
    Neighborhood of Poverty   149

Chapter Twelve
Can You Still Retire Comfortably?:
    Retirement Was Overrated, Anyway   163

Chapter Thirteen
The End Game: "If Something Cannot
    Go on Forever, It Will Stop"   181

So Long, Farewell   197

Acknowledgments   201

About the Authors   203

Check In with the
Control Tower

HERE IS THE FINANCIAL PROFILE of many people you know:

In 2007, Americans had a zero savings rate and totally inadequate savings to put against the liabilities they will face over the course of their prolonged retirements. After the market panic and the recession of 2008–2009, what little savings they had were drastically reduced (even though the savings rate rose above zero), alongside the value of their biggest single asset—the equity in their homes—vaporizing nearly everyone's plans for a serene retirement. This means many Americans are going to be opting for the Hindu ideal, where old people forsake all worldly possessions, pick up a begging bowl, and wander the streets. Except in our case, it won't be voluntary.

We are sliding down this road on greased skids. If we do nothing more than follow the dictates of our heart and our culture, it will lead us to financial ruin.

As young people, we spend every dollar plus whatever we can put on Visa to buy clothes, cars, cocktails, vacations, dinners, and entertainment. Our pocketbook is small but our wants are great. Why shouldn't we have it all?

Then, as middle-agers, our wages increase but our needs expand even faster. We need McMansions and sports-utility vehicles. We need designer furniture. We need to send our kids to private schools. We need significant, broadening travel. We also may have to kick in to support our own aging parents.

By the time we retire, the piggy bank is empty. We open our phone bills and realize—*wait a minute*—this is my 401(k)! It's hopelessly inadequate to provide for our needs over the next 35 years. We have our house—*ha-ha*—remortgaged to the hilt, but we can't eat it, and even if we could sell it, we weren't planning to live on the sidewalk. Meanwhile, our employment prospects have winnowed to applying for jobs as Wal-Mart greeters, at least as long as our health holds out. Speaking of health, there's no way Medicare can continue to provide anything like today's level of benefits. It will be more like, "Take two (generic) aspirin and go away on that ice floe (to die)." Social Security will be means-tested, which means many of us won't be cashing those checks, either.

This could be exactly where your life is headed. Right now, you are on a luxurious private jet that is flying you in great style to an airport in a remote third-world country where you will be picked up by a broken-down bus, driven to the mountains, and never heard from again.

Right now, you are on a luxurious private jet that is flying you in great style to an airport in a remote third-world country where you will be picked up by a broken-down bus, driven to the mountains, and never heard from again.

Not where you wanted to go? Then it's time to change course. *The Little Book of Bulletproof Investing* will help you do just that.

One of the biggest problems we face is trying to invest our money so that it grows over time. Without long-term compounding of our investment returns—making money off the money we save—our savings will never grow enough to finance our long-term goals.

Here's the problem in a nutshell.

Our Broken Financial System

Imagine that you live next door to a family that takes a big Las Vegas vacation every year. Some years, they hit the jackpot. They buy a new top-of-the-line Lexus, send their kids to private schools, and join a country club. They collect art and wine, and fill their closets with the latest of everything. Their lifestyle is the envy of the neighborhood.

Other years, though, they lose their shirts at the black-jack table. They come home and have to sell the Lexus to buy an old junker. They resign from the country club and pull their kids from the private schools. They sell their art and jewelry at fire-sale prices. Now they buy their clothes at thrift shops, eat cornflakes for dinner, and have bill collectors calling at all hours. Every time you see them, they seemed ground down by worry and anxiety.

If you knew them well enough, you might take them aside and say, "Stop the insanity! Why do you live this way?"

To which they would reply, "Yeah, but next year is gonna be different. We're gonna make it all back."

Gentle reader, you and I are that family next door. This is exactly how we run our investment portfolio. Like Sisyphus, we roll our portfolio up a mountain, only to watch it roll down the other side. Then we do it again. We've done this twice in the last decade alone. This is a long and painful route to nowhere, least of all to a financially secure retirement.

If someone had told us back in October 2007, when the Dow Jones Industrial Average was around 14,000, that we would soon see the stock market crash into the mid-6,000 range—which, adjusted for inflation, is down by almost as much as it was during the Great Depression—we wouldn't have believed it possible.

If someone had told us that at the same time we would see the value of our personal real estate holdings dwindle to "unsaleable at any price," we would have scoffed.

If someone had told us that in the coming year, General Electric, General Motors, Bank of America, and Citibank would sell virtually as penny stocks; that Bear Stearns, Merrill Lynch, Washington Mutual, Wachovia, AIG, and GM would become virtually insolvent; and that Lehman Brothers would simply disappear, we would have said that this person was crazy.

Yet all of this has happened.

If you didn't lose a lot of money during the Panic of 2008, you were probably doing something wrong.

If you didn't lose a lot of money in 2008, you were investing in some extremely unusual fashion. Possibly, you had a portfolio of T-bills, which is to say, you were not investing at all. Possibly, you held a portfolio of long-term government bonds, which did super-well in 2008 but means you have subsequently lost a lot of money and are poised to do badly going forward. Possibly, you own nothing but gold, in which case you are a survivalist and have bought one of the worst performing investments in recent decades. Or, possibly, you are a follower of some short-term market-timing system that has you making wild swings in and out of the market in a way that cannot work in the long run for the simple reason that no one can see the future.

If you didn't lose a lot of money during the Panic of 2008, you were probably doing something wrong.

If you fall into one of the above categories, you probably feel like a genius, but in truth all you have been is incredibly lucky. You were in the Men's Room when the bus left that drove off a cliff. That doesn't mean you are going to get to where you want to go.

The long-term implications of this panic are devastating for a Boomer generation on the cusp of retirement. The traders, speculators, hedge funds, and government have dealt contemptuously with those of us who were saving and investing for our future security. Because the market didn't appear to be valued at ridiculously high levels (say, as it was in 2000), it seemed perfectly prudent to invest in the stock market. Then the rug was pulled out from under us.

We subsequently watched the government fumble as it tried to solve the problem it largely created. This was like sending Godzilla into Tokyo to fight Rodan (the monster, not to be confused with Rodin, the sculptor). We don't know who is going to win, but we bet there is going to be a lot of collateral damage.

Our financial system is broken. By this, we are not referring to the global institutions that got us into the present crisis, although these obviously have their issues. Nor are we referring to outright fraud and market manipulation, though there has been plenty of that as well. Rather, we mean the system by which the ordinary citizen invests in the capital markets. He is promised safety and security and total returns. Instead, he finds a river full of crocodiles. The financial services industry has failed to engineer a solution that manages wealth in a way that addresses both people's short-term ability to withstand loss as well as their long-term need for capital appreciation.

Jeremy Siegel's classic *Stocks for the Long Run* examines U.S. stock market performance from 1801 to 2001 and concludes that, after inflation, stocks have returned almost 7 percent per year over this period. Yet no sooner do we reach for these fruits than the boughs of the tree recede from us. Frustratingly, we cannot take this 7 percent to the bank. If we buy in near a market peak, decades may pass before we realize a 7 percent return on our own investments—during which time we can watch our portfolio be sliced in half along the way. We invest for the long run, but we still have to eat every day. John Maynard Keynes said that in the long run we are all dead. Unfortunately, Keynes's long run can catch up to us before Siegel's does.

Here, then, is the investor's paradox: We need the maximum return we can get from our investment dollar in order to compound the giant sums of money required to support us through our retirement. However, if we go for the big returns, we inevitably risk taking a big hit that substantially wipes out our savings. On the other hand, if we forgo the high returns by avoiding stocks, our nest egg never grows. We need to find a better way of getting the returns we need without the risk that will destroy our savings before we get there. That is another goal of this book.

Really Bad Scenarios

If we have managed to lose one-quarter to one-half of our money living in a land of plenty during relatively good times, it does not take great powers of imagination to see that things could have been worse. Seriously bad economic times occur in more places and more often than one might think: Norway, Finland, and Sweden during the early 1990s; Japan throughout the 1990s; Hong Kong, Singapore, South Korea, and Taiwan in 1997; Russia in 1998; Argentina in 2001; Iceland in 2008. Some of these are countries with significant economies. Researchers have identified 38 crises in 27 industrialized countries from 1970 to 1999. This list does not even include the sub-Saharan African states ravaged by war and civil strife, where daily life is unthinkable by U.S. standards.

Who can say what economic scenarios will unfold between now and the end of our lives? We have no control over the future direction of the stock market. We have no control over the future direction of interest rates. We have no control over the business cycle or the economy. We have no control over China or Iran. The list of things that are beyond our understanding and control is nearly endless. While we cannot control the outcome, we can control our strategy. We can try to prepare intelligently for this unknown future.

A Man, a Plan, a Canal: Panama

Okay, forget Panama and you don't need a canal, but you do need a plan: a lifetime financial plan. Earlier generations didn't, because they smoked and drank hard and died young without having 35 years of retirement to slog through. Today we live longer. Longevity is a good problem to have, considering the alternative, but it isn't cheap. Instead of a lifetime's worth of savings having to last for 10 or 15 years, now it has to last more like 30 or 40.

This is a book about what you should do (and should not do) as an investor to bulletproof your investments and protect yours savings. Your authors wish we had read such a book when we began our investing careers, since most of these lessons have been taken out of our hides.

Here is the plan:

1. We are going to talk about investor psychology, and show how Wall Street takes advantage of it.
2. Then, we are going to lay out a specific investing program that focuses on limiting your downside risk—and we have lit up a website (www.tangentportfolio .com) to help you set it up.
3. We will offer strategies for maximizing your income and savings throughout your financial life.
4. Finally, we have peppered the book with Do's and Don'ts that should save you a lot of money, and bulleted them at the end of each chapter.

Our hero, Ben Franklin, wrote, "Experience keeps a dear [expensive] school, but fools will learn in no other." Your authors have lifetime charter memberships in this school. Driven by greed and fear, time and again we have stuck our fingers into electric sockets just to see what would happen. We have learned many dear lessons over our financial lifetimes. Here we pass them along to you dear reader, that your suffering may be less, and your riches greater.

Chapter One

The Nut Behind the Wheel

~

Behavioral Finance in One Lesson

As BEN'S SISTER, Rachel, likes to say, "Your basic human is not such a hot item." Nowhere is this truer than when it comes time for said average human being to manage his or her own investments. To understand what has gone so very wrong with our financial lives, we need to look more closely at the man or woman in the mirror.

Two devils toss investors back and forth between their pitchforks. One of these is *Greed*, and the other is *Fear*. According to this model of investor psychology, the prudent investor is the one who chooses a moderate course, being neither inordinately greedy nor disproportionately fearful. This investor reins in his feelings and threads an Aristotelian mean between these two emotional extremes. There is a lot to be said for this line of thinking, probably because it is true.

If we probe a little deeper, we see that greed and fear are not two emotions, but one, and that single emotion is . . . fear. In fact, greed is not an emotion at all, but rather a moral state (one of the Seven Deadly Sins). Greed springs from fear. We fear that we will not have enough, and so greed overcompensates. At its most primitive level, greed is the fear that the big breast of life will be snatched away, leaving us forever unfilled. Greed can mask social fears as well. We fear not doing as well as our brother-in-law or our next-door neighbor. We may fear that our families will be disappointed with us as providers— that we won't be able to afford that good school, that fancy wedding, that house with the swimming pool.

Why are we so fearful? As Figure 1.1 shows, the brain is like a Tootsie-Roll Pop. The brain stem is the white stick. It is surrounded by a chewy chocolate center, the limbic system, where fear and rage and emotions lurk like a bag of snakes. Finally, it is covered by the cortex, the hard candy shell where thinking occurs. Most of our decisions are emotional

Figure 1.1   The Human Brain

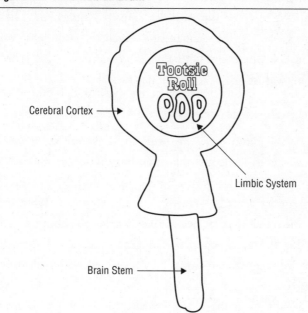

Cerebral Cortex

Limbic System

Brain Stem

at base, and the cortex just makes up reasons to justify them after the fact. This primitive brain wanders through our modern world of fax machines and skyscrapers ever on the lookout for flesh-tearing saurians.

Homo sapiens is a frail, vulnerable creature. Because our thinking and emotions are so enmeshed, it is no surprise that our investing has become confused. So, let's all come up to the front of the tent right now and confess: Investing is terrifying. It is very scary to put our life savings on the line. If the smartest people in the world can manage to screw it up, what chance do we have to come out with our skins still attached? These thoughts lead us into a desperate search for confidence and reassurance where our investing is concerned. This search takes myriad forms. We'll highlight two of them.

The Unwisdom of Crowds

One of the main ways we seek to allay our fears when we invest is to seek safety in numbers. If everyone else is doing it, at least we won't be out on a limb by ourselves. Unfortunately, this strategy doesn't work. Everyone piles into the market when the market is highest, and dives for the exits when the market is lowest. Following the crowd means following a "buy high, sell low" philosophy that produces the worst results of all.

Crowds have their own distinct patterns of behavior that are inimical to investors.

First, crowds engage in *groupthink*—the tendency for everyone in a group to think alike. Mobs move to a consensus and then squash dissent. Anyone who questions the consensus view is held out for social ridicule.

Second, crowds display something called *response polarization*. This means that nuanced responses get washed out in favor of starkly black-or-white, simplistic choices. A stock or an investing idea is viewed as being either all good or all bad.

Third, crowds show a *risky shift*. This is the "lynch mob" effect. Taken singly, people are unlikely to storm the Sheriff's office to string up Black Bart. Once in a group, however, they feel invincible. Groups are likely to adapt more extreme positions than individual members would take individually.

All these tendencies undercut the wisdom of crowds.

There are famous examples where individuals guess the weight of a pig or the number of jellybeans in a jar, and the group estimates turn out to be astonishingly accurate. This is the basis for *efficient market theory*, which contends that all actors in aggregate have a better fix on the price of, say, Microsoft, than any individual participant is likely to have. However, in the case of the jellybeans, the estimates were made singly, with no consultation among participants. In the case of stock prices, the guesses of all other actors are known, and their value, direction, and momentum serve as anchors for each next guess. This amplifies price swings far in excess of what is justified by stock fundamentals, and accounts for the manic-depressive moods of the stock market (or "Mr. Market," as the investing genius Benjamin Graham personified it). Think of how much better it feels to buy a stock on an "up" day when everyone on TV is smiling and happy than on a big "down" day when the anchors are somber and grim. Yet, you do far better when buying low.

Bottom line: Do not trust the Force when investing. John Bogle, founder of Vanguard Group and patron saint of investors, was able to estimate the cost of investing according to our feelings. He found that, from 1980 to 2005, buying high and selling low cost investors 2.7 percent annually over a simple buy-and-hold strategy. Our emotions are at best a contrary indicator, leading us to do the opposite of what we should. That is investing psychology in one sentence.

Do not trust the Force when investing. Our emotions are at best a contrary indicator, leading us to do the opposite of what we should.

Our Portfolios, Ourselves

A second way we search for security in securities is by buying stocks that are cool, like our cars and our clothes. We are, after all, what we own.

In 2000, people bought CMGI for $137 a share (adjusted for splits). Today it sells for $1.59, for a loss of 99 percent of your original investment. That same year, you could have bought Sycamore Networks (SCMR) for $171; now it's at $3.79, for a loss of 98 percent. If you loved Palm (PALM) at $1,084, you must be thrilled to be able to buy more today for $26.57 (a loss of 98 percent). People who thought i2 Technologies (ITWO) was going to the moon at $2,600 a share can find more today for $18, for a loss of 99 percent of their initial investment.

CMGI, you will recall, was the famous incubator of Internet companies that was going to rule e-commerce (and in the World of Tomorrow, was there really going to be any other kind?). Sycamore Networks provided seamless optical integration of e-business networks and processes to optimize their data infrastructure. Palm makes the ubiquitous digital assistants that are nothing if not an extension of our nervous systems. i2 Technologies is a software company that revolutionizes supply chain management.

Free association time: What adjectives come to mind when we think of these companies from the standpoint of 1999? Hot? Sexy? Fast? High energy? New? Smart? Futuristic? Feel free to make your own list.

Now consider some different companies: Hormel, they make Spam; Altria, purveyors of death in the form of tobacco; Arch Coal, they make coal. How do these companies rank on the same continuum we just constructed? Perhaps such words as "*bor-ring*," "yesterday's news," and "just say no" come to mind. If you were going to a cocktail party in January 2000, would you rather be able to say you worked for i2 Technologies or Arch Coal? One business card would lead to waking up the next morning in a suite at the Plaza with an empty bottle of Dom Perignon on one side and a blonde on the other, while the guy with the other card ends up at home by nine watching a *Love Boat* rerun with a bag of Cheetos.

However, if you'd bought any of these boring companies that month, you would be far richer as of 2009: Hormel is up 110 percent, Altria is up 366 percent, and Arch Coal is up 738 percent. Today, it's the guy from Arch Coal who gets the girl (she knows he can keep her warm).

We buy stocks that are a reflection of our ego ideal.

The problem is that everyone else is doing the same thing. This means we are paying a big premium to invest in companies like these. When we buy groovy companies, we are not paying for a hamburger today but for a hamburger next Tuesday. We can see it, we can taste it, but it's not exactly in the bun yet. We know how Spam is selling already—there's very little mystery left—but the sky's the limit when it comes to thinking how big that company in China is going to get. It can be as big as your imagination.

What happens next? It turns out that we have overpaid for our sexy growth stocks. The earnings don't materialize as we dreamed they would (and paid a price to match). On the other hand, we weren't expecting much from Altria or Hormel to begin with, so we didn't overpay for them. This is why the Brandes Institute found that stodgy large-cap U.S. value stocks (more about these later) outperformed large-cap "glamour" stocks by 6.8 percent annually from 1968 to 2008. Our investing narcissism has a price.

This brings us to our little list of Investment Psychology Do's and Don'ts.

Investment Psychology Do's and Don'ts

Here are some better ideas than investing to be hip, slick, and cool.

DO aim low.

As in any 12-step program, the first step is to realize that we are powerless over the market. However smart we are, we cannot control how our investments will perform, no matter how much we study and prepare. There are always larger forces at work.

This means we should aim low. The lower our aspirations, the more likely it is that we will achieve them. It is seldom a good idea to make any "bold" investment decisions. The market exists to teach us bone-crunching lessons in humility. You can lose real money there. Investments that will give you big returns without commensurate big risks are like Elvis sightings: intriguing, perhaps, but seldom verified.

DO be patient.

Our time horizon is the rest of our lives, not next week or next quarter. Our goal should be to harvest the long-term positive returns flowing from global capitalism—a proven and profitable economic system.

The market pays us to assume stress. If we wanted to eliminate stress, we would earn the returns of T-bills. Of course, this would lead to its own form of stress later on, when the time comes to retire, because our nest egg would not grow enough to support us later in life. We need to take on more stress from our investments today so we can have less financial stress in our lives later.

DON'T panic or be elated over short-term market events.

There is no advantage to being a "hot reactor" and working ourselves into a lather over breaking news and market events. Feelings come and feelings go, and feelings are not facts. Our tendency is to take today's headlines and rush down the field with them to some horrible or wonderful goalpost. Selling in a panic can destroy a lifetime of investing returns. The news can be grim day after day and the world is coming to an end, and then suddenly, when no one expects it, the news is good and the robins are singing and what was all the fuss about, anyway?

Investors overreact to good and bad times alike, and over-extrapolate from short-term trends into the future. We have a poster from Dimensional Fund Advisors—one of the top investment advisory firms that has ever been— showing a timeline for the past 100 years with news head-lines pasted over it. These events include: "World War I," "Communist Revolution," "Influenza Pandemic," "Stock Market Crash of '29," "Great Depression," "Pearl Harbor," "Sputnik Launched," "JFK Assassinated," "Arab Oil Embargo," "Disco," "Stock Market Crash of '87," "Gulf War," "September 11th," and so on. Over this is a corresponding chart of the stock market, which climbs at about a 45-degree angle throughout the century in seeming disregard of all the disasters that befell us. From the point of view of a long-term investor (and all of us are lifelong investors, now), these crises proved to be terrible times to sell stocks. If you think that because you despair about the state of the civilization (your authors' chronic condition) it follows that you ought to liquidate your portfolio, think again.

Next up: A look at what is Ground Zero in many ways.

Do's and Don'ts

- Don't trust the Force when investing. Your emotions are contra-indicators of what you should do.

- Don't invest in companies because you think they are sexy and cool or because you want to be cool.

- Do approach the market with great humility and realize that you are powerless over the market.

- Do be patient. The market pays you to assume stress.

- Don't get hopped up over short-term market events, despite the media's attempt to whip you into a frenzy.

Chapter Two

Wall Street Therapy

~

For Good and for Evil

IF WE HUMAN BEINGS ARE WEAK, impressionable creatures desperately looking for a little guidance where our investing is concerned, perhaps there is someone who can help us out a little. We have a lot of money; we just need someone to give us a helping hand. Is that too much to ask?

Welcome to Wall Street, the place where the "two to take him" (as in "a sucker born every minute and two to take him") live.

Unfortunately, entrance into this world does not mean that our problems are over; in fact, they probably have gotten worse. Before, we were struggling in waters over our heads. Now, we look down to see we are in a shark tank.

Here's how it works. Readers of a certain age will recall the three ego states from Eric Berne's *Games People Play*:

1. **Parent Ego State:** Contains all the parental messages we heard growing up
2. **Adult Ego State:** Our logical information-processing tool for dealing with the outside world
3. **Child Ego State:** The kid who still lives inside each of us

Figure 2.1 diagrams the three ego states (Parent-Adult-Child) in a typical adult-to-adult transaction between a Wall Street financial professional and a client. Notice how investing is an adult-ego-state, thinking-oriented activity, with little role for either the parent or child ego states.

When it comes to investing, however, our parent and adult ego states are a little shaky, leaving our inner child feeling frightened and confused. This sets up the classic investing countertransference. Figure 2.2 holds a fluoroscope up to the transaction in Figure 2.1. As you can see, Wall Street authority figures and experts take over for the

Figure 2.1   Adult-to-Adult Investing Conversation

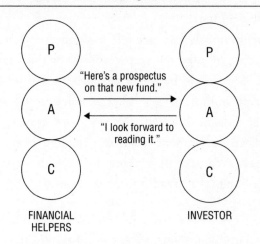

Figure 2.2   What's Really Going On

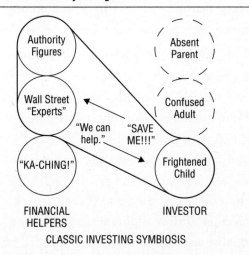

investor, combining to make one ("you and us") symbiotic psychological unit.

Unconsciously, we are all looking for a surrogate parent who will take the responsibility for our investment choices. This might be a market guru on TV or the curmudgeonly author of a market newsletter. It can be a confident stockbroker with the world on a string or the gray-haired investment advisor who has been around the block. We are all looking for the stronger, more confident one (aka "Dad") to reassure us.

Unconsciously, we are all looking for a surrogate parent who will take the responsibility for our investment choices.

We are forever looking to the expert who is smarter than we are to figure it all out for us. Wall Street provides gurus and wizards galore who are happy to take this burden off our shoulders. Nothing is easier than for a pundit to pick two data points out of a hat, connect the dots, and make a prediction about the future based on which way they point. Or, they can point to a black-box trading system that turns investing into rocket science, or a hedge fund manager with a reputation for being a genius, or the mutual fund with the best returns in its category last month, quarter, year, or past five years. There's always a show. *See Jo-Jo, the dog-faced boy! Come on inside!*

Wall Street uses its money, power, and prestige to capture your assets (by flattery or intimidation), etherize you on the table, and pick your pockets. The focus is always kept on the markets, never on the man behind the curtain. Investment advisor William Bernstein has calculated that, if we have a full-service wrap account at a name-brand brokerage firm, in 23 years they will have more of our money than we do. These Beagle Boys don't break in and clean out our money bin all at once. They do it one drip at a time, keeping the patient alive (if comatose) as long as possible. Meanwhile, they hide in steel-and-glass office buildings behind mahogany desks and Bloomberg screens, fire off impossible-to-interpret statements, and print quarterly newsletters full of stock market doubletalk to make sure we feel ignorant and confused, too intimidated and afraid of showing our ignorance to ask questions, and, above all, in need of their ongoing help. Of course, their primary goal is to help themselves, not us.

Unfortunately, though, all of us need some help. For starters, we need a lifetime financial plan. There is no way to figure out an overall financial game plan on our own. There are just too many variables to keep track of, let alone all their interactions. We need to know about state and federal tax rates. We need to know about benefit programs. We need to plug in our housing needs, present and future. Vacation home? College? Wedding? They all go in here, too. We need to estimate the future course of our earnings and our investment returns, and make sure everything is adjusted for inflation. This is not easy. Most of us have enough trouble just figuring out what we're going to have for dinner.

When it comes to generating this master financial plan, the world quickly sorts itself into two types of people: do-it-yourselfers, and those who turn to professional experts for help. Do-it-yourselfers will do well to use a program like *ESPlanner* (www.esplanner.com) to crunch the numbers. Others will want to find a *Certified Financial Planner* (*CFP*) who will use similar software to work up this document.

Becoming a Grownup

Whether you do it yourself, or find someone to develop the plan for you, you want a document that shows, with some reasonable probability of success, how your retirement will be funded. The same goes for the other big-ticket events in your life: college educations, weddings, round-the-world cruises, long-term health care, and so on. Retirement is the Big Kahuna, though. Most of the other items on the wish list are discretionary to some degree.

This whole exercise is about as much fun as having electroshock therapy. Instead of living paycheck-to-paycheck with no thought of tomorrow, suddenly tomorrow comes into focus with dazzling clarity. While painful, this is actually a good thing. When you confront this problem at age 70, your only option is to eat less and cut pills in half. By tackling the problem earlier, your options widen considerably. You henceforth will be living as a grownup who takes responsibility for his or her life, and not as some 45-year-old Peter Pan. Most people you know fall into this latter category, even if they earn more money than you do.

You henceforth will be living as a grownup who takes responsibility for his or her life, not as some 45-year-old Peter Pan.

Of course, just because you have a plan doesn't mean that things will go according to plan. A plan is no better than the assumptions on which it is based. The global economy nearly collapsed in 2008 due to the assumptions of the risk management models in the hands of the brightest people in finance. Your plan will probably have a lot of pseudo-precision, given the inherent uncertainty of many of the inputs. Just because the plan will not be perfect does not mean we should have no plan at all and go to the beach. That is a plan for disaster.

Implementing the Plan

Once you have a plan, you have to *live* the plan. Partly this means earning and saving, about which we will have much to say later. It also means investing your savings intelligently.

Investing is fraught with peril. This remains true whether you invest on your own or through the intermediary of a broker or investment advisor. While in theory, being a do-it-yourselfer is a fine, money-saving idea, in practice it can prove an expensive mistake. This is because there are no checks and balances, and you have the power to destroy everything you have worked for with a few mouse clicks. Against this, while it is possible to find a financial advisor who won't take you to the cleaners, it is much harder than finding a good financial planner. The planner will be guided by a sophisticated software program. Not so with your investment advisor. Naturally, we have a few thoughts on this delicate subject of finding a good financial advisor.

The first step is to completely ignore what kind of car he drives or how expensive his clothes or wristwatch or offices are. This is all for show.

While we are cynical about professional designations, people with a *CFA* after their name (*chartered financial analyst*) will know the difference between Monte Carlo and Monty Python. There are many fine advisors who lack this designation, and there are undoubtedly advisors who do have this designation who are completely unscrupulous. But it does show intellectual mastery of the core content in the area.

There are generally two types of people out to manage your money: *registered investment advisors* and *registered reps* (*stockbrokers*). Investment advisors are typically compensated by charging you a fee based on the assets they manage, while stockbrokers earn commissions on the products they sell you. Another difference is that registered investment advisors are held to be fiduciaries who are supposed to treat your money as more important than their own, putting your interests first. Stockbrokers, on the other hand, need only find investments that are "suitable," which of course can mean anything and so means nothing (although the law on this is changing right now and may be different by the time you read this).

We don't doubt that there are as many terrific stockbrokers as there are lousy registered investment advisors. The truth remains that you cannot afford to ignore how your financial advisors are compensated. People who charge you a fee for their services generally are going to be more careful shoppers on your behalf. It can be difficult to get impartial advice from someone who is incentivized to sell you particular high-margin financial products. As Berkshire Hathaway's Charlie Munger puts it, "If someone presents you with an investment idea that's supposed to make you a lot of money, and there's also a big commission attached for him in the deal, how difficult is it to throw it in the wastebasket?" We take his point.

Whomever you use, your financial advisor should look at your life situation and devise a highly diversified asset allocation that is appropriate to your investment goals. This will probably be some basic pie-chart portfolio. He or she should make sure that your investments are relatively tax-efficient and low-expense, that they are housed in the appropriate types of accounts, and that they don't drift too far from your target allocation. Your advisor also monitors your performance and shows you clearly how you are doing. He or she takes care of day-to-day account servicing: placing trades, making distributions, keeping track of tax costs, and so forth.

While you and the advisor may both think that he earns his money by asset allocation and account servicing, that is not really true. Nor does he earn his keep by finding you brilliant, market-beating investments, or by taking you to cash before the next recession. No one can do those things except by luck, and relying on luck is a poor investment strategy.

A Hymn to Financial Advisors

The advisor's real job is to protect you from yourself. He will try to talk you out of all the screwball investing ideas that you will get from time to time. These ideas are constantly being churned up by the financial media. Unless you completely tune out this circus, unless you ignore all the cocktail party chatter, you will be susceptible. As economist Charles Kindleberger noted, "There is nothing so disturbing to one's well-being and judgment as to see a friend get rich." You will abandon what you were doing, which was perfectly sensible, and do something stupid instead. Cut loose from your moorings, you will bounce from one bogus investment idea to the next. It will be a long road back, and you will hitchhike home wearing a barrel.

The advisor's other main job is to keep you from jumping out the window when the market starts delaminating, and to hold a steadying hand on the tiller to keep you on course toward your goals. Selling out at a market bottom is tantamount to committing financial suicide. As Dimensional Fund's Daniel Wheeler points out, bailing out does not even solve the psychological problem that was the root cause of the error in the first place. A week after you go to cash, when the market is up 2 percent, you still lie in bed wondering—*did I make a mistake?* Then the market goes down 2 percent and you lie in bed thinking: *I guess I did the right thing after all—or did I?* Then the market goes up 2 percent, and so on. Going to cash does not stop the self-torture.

A good advisor will do the same for your spouse and kids after you kick off to join the heavenly choir, which means your family will not be left at the mercy of the slick financial predators who are guaranteed to descend on them at their most vulnerable time, intent on capturing your life savings.

The advisor does not do this for free; his fees or commissions are subtracted from your returns. This means that over time your returns will lag those of the market. However, you can still do better this way than if you had been managing your money on your own, because what he really did was help you and your family avoid all the roads not taken that would have led to financial disaster.

Investment Advice Do's and Don'ts

DO control what you can.

Instead of trying to control what is beyond your control, such as the future of the global economy, your efforts would be better directed toward controlling those few simple things that you can.

One such thing is your investment fees and expenses. These include, but are not limited to: commissions to buy and sell stocks, account fees, wrap fees, advisor fees, mutual fund expenses, 12-b fees, loads, and so on. Every penny spent on these fees is a penny out of your pocket. Over an investment lifetime, it adds up to a fortune.

The second thing you can control is your asset allocation: the ratio of stocks to bonds to other things in your portfolio. This will help you roughly size up what you might expect in the way of investment returns over the long run, as well as how big a risk you are taking along the way to get them.

Third, you can control the extent to which your holdings are diversified. You need to own *asset classes* whose performance does not correlate with each other—especially during a market panic, when all correlations tend to converge. We all thought that the standard pie chart portfolio we owned was plenty diversified, until 2008 taught us differently. More on this later.

Paying attention to these three issues will lead you to invest in broad market index funds—funds that track indexes like the S&P 500, the MSCI EAFE index of foreign stocks from developed nations, the MSCI Emerging Markets index, as well as index funds in other categories. These will help you broadly diversify while minimizing the expenses of financial intermediaries.

DON'T listen to investment media.

CNBC patterns itself after its even more successful twin, ESPN. That may be a smart way to run a TV station, but buying stocks as a competitive sport is not a smart way to frame your investing. There is no need for a jockstrap. It is not about winners and losers and a clock counting down in hundredths of a second. This psychs us up for the big win. The goal of investing is usually to maximize our lifetime state of wealth. Whether or not we bought 10 shares of Google at the initial public offering is not really going to affect this very much. Remember that all these media are paid for by the financial services industry. Their interest is in hooking us into the game.

The goal of investing is to maximize our lifetime state of wealth.

The fact that there is an investing show going on 24 hours a day does not mean that the average investor will profit from focusing on its activity. It is a giant distraction and will only tempt you into reckless action. You don't worry about how much your house or your business or your labor is worth from hour to hour—why is it important to pay that much attention to your stocks? This kind of micro-attention is counterproductive.

DON'T go to sleep.

No matter whom you may hire, the main person watching out for your money has to be you. When you open an investment account, all those papers you sign basically say, "Abandon hope, all ye who enter here." Supposedly this is being reformed, but don't hold your breath. If something goes wrong, it will be your money and your peace of mind that are gone. You will be able to write angry letters but it won't bring your money back.

DON'T be a snob.

If you are a high-net-worth type, you need to be extremely careful with your money. The industry hunts fatted calves to extinction, using subtle appeals to status and vanity. If you succumb, you will be taught a severe lesson in humility. Most rich people would be a lot richer if they bypassed the private banking department and invested alongside Joe Sixpack in a few index funds at Vanguard.

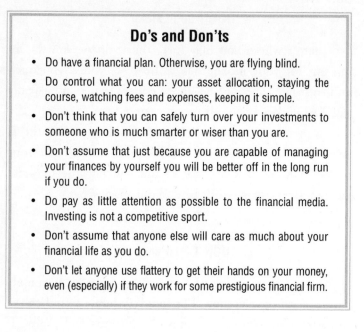

Do's and Don'ts

- Do have a financial plan. Otherwise, you are flying blind.

- Do control what you can: your asset allocation, staying the course, watching fees and expenses, keeping it simple.

- Don't think that you can safely turn over your investments to someone who is much smarter or wiser than you are.

- Don't assume that just because you are capable of managing your finances by yourself you will be better off in the long run if you do.

- Do pay as little attention as possible to the financial media. Investing is not a competitive sport.

- Don't assume that anyone else will care as much about your financial life as you do.

- Don't let anyone use flattery to get their hands on your money, even (especially) if they work for some prestigious financial firm.

Chapter Three

How Not to Invest

~

Kids, Don't Try This at Home

An experimenter divided his subjects into two groups and gave them the same difficult task. Each group had to look through a microscope and discriminate which of two types of cells they were looking at. Neither group had any prior knowledge of how to do this.

The group in the first room received accurate feedback on their performance, and after making a lot of wrong guesses, gradually began to improve. When they reached a point where they started to get the answers right, the experimenter stopped them.

The group in the second room received purely random feedback. The professor would flip a coin and tell them if they were right or wrong depending on whether "heads" or "tails" came up. Not surprisingly, this group's performance did not improve. However, they developed extremely complicated and elaborate theories to justify their guesses.

The instructor then brought the groups together to discuss their conclusions. What happened? The second group, whose answers were complicated but wrong, convinced the first group, whose answers were simple but mostly correct, that they were mistaken. The first group became seduced by the more complex (if fanciful and incorrect) view.

If the two groups had been studying investing instead of looking at slides, the outcome would have been the same. What few good investment ideas are out there would be sidelined by the many terrible ideas crowding the field.

When you mix our basic human insecurity with Wall Street's desire to make a buck, the resulting Kool-Aid can be hazardous to your wealth. Here is a little list of what we know that doesn't work. All of these approaches have been tried—in many cases, by your authors personally— and have failed. They are like 40 miles of bad road, and you would do well to detour around them.

Be Smarter than Everyone Else (Ha Ha)

One way to make a lot of money in the stock market is to be smarter than everyone else. Sure, there may be dozens of analysts with MBAs studying a given stock full time, and millions of investors and billions of dollars riding on its performance. Sure, all this information is digested into the stock's price on a second-by-second basis. But don't underestimate yourself. You are probably smarter than them.

DO take your time.

Efficient Market Theory says that the stock market *quickly* incorporates all available information into the price of a stock. Brokerage firms pay a lot of money to house their supercomputers right next to the stock market so that their trades can arrive *nanoseconds faster* than others'. However, you have plenty of time to read and digest information about a stock and still get there ahead of everyone else.

Let's say you are in the dentist's office and you pick up last month's copy of *Forbes* magazine. Let's say further that it has an article about some nimble biotech company whose new treatment for heart disease has passed Phase 3 clinical trials. Think about it. Everyone has a heart. If this drug works, it could be worth zillions. As soon as the dentist has finished drilling, go home and buy 1,000 shares or 10,000 shares. It's not as if everyone else reacted to this information within moments of the announcement, the week before *Forbes* went to press. Who knows—the company might have another drug in the pipeline that will work, too. This way you will get in on the action before anyone even knows about it.

DO find a brilliant, prestigious financial advisor like Bernard Madoff or John Stanford.

There's nothing to worry about—after all, the SEC must monitor these guys. Even if by some stroke of misfortune you do end up with a crook, the government will undoubtedly make you whole by sending a big-ticket check from "U.S. Treasury" straight to your bank account. Relax— that check is in the mail.

Give all your money to somebody who will also take custody of your assets personally. You don't want an advisor who uses a name-brand custodian like Fidelity or Schwab or Ameritrade to hold your assets, a custodian that might also have an interest in protecting its own reputation and making sure everything is on the up-and-up. You don't want the ability to verify independently what is in your account by going directly to the custodian. Your advisor probably has a custodian he already likes in the Cayman Islands.

———————————— ∾ ————————————

Give all your money to someone who will take custody of your assets personally.

It's also best if he handles the performance reporting to let you know how you're doing. After all, in these days when everyone uses manual typewriters and abacuses, it's practically impossible to print a piece of paper with a column of made-up numbers saying something that isn't true. If it has a pie chart and three-color graphics, then it must be especially true. Why would you want some firm you have heard of auditing your returns?

What's that? You don't have the millions it takes to attract this kind of high-priced Wall Street talent—at least, not yet? Not a problem, you can get the same thing for a couple of hundred bucks:

DO subscribe to market newsletters.

You won't believe how difficult it is to start a stock market newsletter. For example, you need a computer and a printer, and that's just for openers. You might even need a website and an 800 number. Only the elite need apply.

It makes total sense that anyone who had uncovered a system for beating the market—insights worth billions of dollars—would sell it to you for $199 a year. It turns out that that token $199 they want is just a cover charge to keep out the riff-raff. The investment newsletters are all run by philanthropists.

---— ∾ ———

It makes total sense that anyone who had uncovered a system for beating the market would sell it to you for $199 a year.

Here's a tip that will help you weed out the great newsletters from the merely good ones. Make sure they advertise a track record of amazing, market-stomping returns that you might have obtained if you had only been smart enough to start subscribing five years earlier. These track records are carefully audited and if it's in a newsletter, you can bet the SEC stands behind every word.

But what if you are a little short on cash this month and can't come up with the subscription to the market newsletter? Not to worry. Great advice is as close as your TV dial.

DO pay great attention to those pundits on TV.

Fortunately for you, if a guy or gal is on TV, you can bet that he or she is a big-time expert who has been carefully vetted. Probably these people have serious training and credentials as economists and a record of accurate predictions. True, the networks have hours and hours of empty programming to fill every day that stretch out like the sands of the Kalahari, but this would never cause them to lower their standards.

These pundits invariably have your best interests at heart. Most of them have no affiliation with the financial services industry. They would never try to talk up a position they held (so they could sell it out from under you) or badmouth a position their firm was shorting. The experts from the government and the think tanks have no agenda, either. Believe everything they tell you.

Keep a pencil and paper by the TV, so you will never miss their valuable guidance. Whenever people have really valuable inside information, the first thing they always do is give it away free on TV.

While being brilliant is a sure way to make a lot of money in the stock market, it's by no means the only way, as we shall see.

Be Clairvoyant

You might think that to predict the future accurately, you would have to be able to predict the outcome of political elections, the direction of the economy, interest rates, world events, and so forth, and shake all these together in one Magic Eight Ball. This sounds like it might be tough, but in practice it turns out to be pretty easy.

DO practice technical analysis.

Take a look at a chart of a stock's performance. Do you see it going down, day after day, for weeks at a time, right down the drain? This means it's a dog and you should sell it or even short it. On the other hand, is the stock going up? Up and up and then up some more, and then up again after that? This is a good stock. Back up the truck.

This approach is called *technical analysis* and you need to spend a lot of time studying its higher mysteries. For some reason, the deepest thinkers in finance all gravitate here. Best of all, you can trade stocks this way all day long without having the slightest idea what you are doing. If a stock starts to go down, sell it and get on the elevator with another one that's going up. If you only own stocks that are going up, you cannot lose.

But wait—there's more! A recent academic study shows that people who do the *opposite* of the above actually make even more money. If you do both at once, your portfolio will be perfectly hedged and you should do the best of all.

If looking at stock charts sounds boring, there is a convenient back door into the future:

DO study those quarterly wrap-ups of top-performing stocks and mutual funds.

If you are ever lucky enough to lay your hands on one of those quarterly wrap-ups of stock and mutual fund performance—especially those that list all the top stocks and mutual funds you might have owned if only you had known the future—this is like having a goldmine delivered right to your door. Since we know the future is going to be just like the past, all you have to do is buy yesterday's top performers and then—*whoa!*—hang on to your hat. What goes up must keep going up, as the saying goes.

In some cases, these lists will have ratings of the top mutual funds, ranging from one to five stars. If they have five stars, you cannot help but make a lot of money. This means the rating agency Morningstar has done all the work for you, and luckily for you this company has the ability to see into the future. It can't be that their top-rated funds routinely are trounced by index funds, can it? It can't be that recently their 1-star funds ended up beating their 5-star funds, can it? No; buy all 5-star funds immediately. Once you have a list of last quarter's top performing stocks and mutual funds, the only other thing you will need to cash in on this information is a time machine.

~

Once you have a list of last quarter's top-performing stocks and mutual funds, the only other thing you will need to cash in on this information is a time machine.

DO practice day-to-day, short-term market timing.

Instead of being one of those chumps who buy and hold forever, even while the market takes a nosedive, the smart move is to swing in and out of stocks like Tarzan jumping from vine to vine.

It's true that back in 1975, Nobelist William Sharpe wrote a paper that debunked most investors' ability to do this successfully. Sharpe pointed out that every market-timing decision unpacks into two decisions: one to get out, and another to get back in. For the process to be profitable, you have to make both calls correctly. Add in transaction costs, and the odds of making money this way are daunting, said Sharpe. However, as long as you are right more than 83 percent of the time, you will make a bundle this way.

What if you are neither smarter than everyone else nor able to predict the future correctly? Is there any hope for just the average Jack or Jill who doesn't want to devote his or her whole life to it? Of course there is.

Investing—Hobby of Champions

Do you find that you're easily bored? Are you amused by flashing lights on a screen? Do you wish you had more money? Do you enjoy bragging when things go right? Then investing is the perfect hobby for you. All you need is your computer, a TV set, and your life savings. You can just tell this is going to end well. Here are some tips anyone can follow to spend money effortlessly in the stock market:

DON'T know what you're doing?

At least you can do a lot of it. You won't make money if you just let your investments sit there idling. What's fun about that? You have to get out and make something happen. For example, you can buy a programmed trading system that will automatically execute trades for you all day long even while you're playing tennis, and then all night long on foreign exchanges while you sleep. This makes getting rich an effortless process. Notice that hedge funds and actively managed mutual funds are famous for their frequent trades as well—just like you!

DO act on stock tips immediately.

Stock tips have tremendous value. You never know where you might get a good stock tip. A cab driver? On the fairway of the seventh hole? A snatch of conversation overheard at a restaurant? That cute girl who cuts your hair? Just make sure your cell phone is charged so you can phone in your order right on the spot. You'll be amazed how your winnings pile up, tip after tip.

Sometimes the best tips just come in as cold calls. A broker calls saying he can get you in on a land deal. Or, he knows a penny stock that's about to pop. Instead of poking around Internet chat rooms for ideas, once you have an e-mail address, great investment ideas will come to you straight from the cloud.

As you might expect, we've been saving the best for last:

DO goose your investment returns through leverage.

When the market is on a solid uptrend, you can double your investment returns by going on margin—paying the brokerage firm a few pennies to borrow money from them and then shoveling that borrowed money straight back to work in the stock market. If you liked how much your account was going up before, you won't believe how much you'll love levering up those returns. Now you're making money using *other people's* money. How sweet is that? Hedge funds do this all the time, gearing their portfolios 30:1 or even more. It's difficult to imagine how you could ever get into trouble just being levered a measly 2:1.

We should probably put this in a footnote in small type at the end of the book, but—just so we can say we told you, nothing to pay attention to, really—be sure to tell your broker that you want to go *off* margin just before the market goes down. While it won't happen to you, some people have been known to receive unpleasant "margin calls" where the broker has to sell their securities out from under them to raise enough collateral to maintain the loan. No reason to get upset here; the market will turn around eventually . . . and if you're on margin, you'll be poised to reap beaucoup profits when it does.

DO get in on investing fads before it's too late.

There have been some great investing fads in our time and if you missed even one you missed a lot of action. There were the "nifty-fifty" stocks in the 1960s that could never go down. Then they went down. There was gold at nearly $1,000 an ounce in the 1970s. It went to $200 and even after 30 years, it is still just a few percentage points above its high in the late 1970s. Then Japan, Inc. dominated the United States with its inscrutable Zen-like ways. Its recession began in 1990 and lasted a decade. Then Internet stocks created a New Economy that made a mockery out of the old bricks-and-mortar businesses. Can you say, 2001–2002? Then we learned that residential real estate could never go down. Today, there's green technology, China . . . just imagine the upside. If you had bought into all of these fads, just think how rich you would be now.

What's that? You say you *did* buy into all of these fads? Never mind. . . .

Do's and Don'ts

Okay, enough sarcasm! Here's the deal: slow, steady, and boring wins the race.

- Don't assume that you can beat the market by stock picking. Do you know something the market doesn't?
- Don't give any weight to market forecasts. All opinion pro and con is already built into the price of equities today.
- Don't assume that if anyone were genius enough to devise a market-beating strategy he would be stupid enough to share it with anyone.
- Don't think you can successfully engage in short-term market timing.
- Don't look to the stock market for investotainment.
- Do trade as infrequently as possible.
- Don't speculate on stock tips.
- Don't go on margin.
- Don't follow fads.

Chapter Four

How to Invest

~

It's Not as Fun as It Used to Be

STRANGE TO SAY, we know a great deal about what *not* to do when it comes to investing, but only a few positive things about what *to* do. However, these few things are extremely powerful.

Here's the list:

- Simplify.
- Diversify.
- Invest passively and consistently, with an emphasis on the tried and true.

- Minimize expenses and taxes.
- Buy and hold.

Whoever first came up with this deserves a Nobel Prize. Let's take each item one by one, shall we?

Simplify

The simpler your approach to investing, the better. You want to own simple assets that anyone can understand: shares of businesses and debt that has a high probability of being paid back with interest. Extremely complicated financial products can be devised, but they are difficult to analyze and come with high fees. They may be suitable for somebody, but don't assume that person is you, even if someone seems very eager to sell you one.

Diversify

In 1953, a grad student named Harry Markowitz came up with the idea that if you hold a bunch of different investments, you get the average of the returns from all the investments but at less than their average risk, because some will be up while others are down. This insight eventually won him a Nobel Prize. *Diversification* has been called the only free lunch in financial economics. By lowering your risk, it increases your returns, because your portfolio doesn't fall as much during bad times and doesn't have to regain as much lost ground to get ahead during good times.

Invest Passively

The idea of active money management has immediate appeal. Active management means that money managers perform fundamental analysis of securities, technical analysis of price trends, and combine this with their macro outlook for the economy to select just those stocks that are most likely to beat the market. This sounds good, but it rarely works, and works least of all for the ordinary investor. Study after study has demonstrated that buying and holding a passive index fund that owns all the stocks in the market—cats and dogs alike—will beat the active managers most of the time.

How can this be? Since the market is nothing more than the sum of activity by all investors, by definition half of the active managers will fall below average any given year. Tack on their fees, and suddenly the market as a whole outperforms the vast majority. Investment advisor Robert Arnott did a study of active mutual fund managers over a 20-year period and concluded that active investors have about a 15 percent chance of beating a market index fund after fees and taxes. Unfortunately, his study suffered from survivorship bias: He was able to look only at funds that had survived a full 20 years. The database that includes all mutual funds over this period—both dead and alive—lists one dead fund for every two that are still kicking. The funds that failed along the way did not fail because they were incredibly successful. This suggests that the actual number of active managers beating the indexes is south of even Arnott's discouraging estimate of 15 percent.

To make matters worse, there is no consistency as to who wins: Last year's active manager who beat the market after expenses is unlikely to repeat next year. Even the most successful active investor of all time, Warren Buffett, thinks that a long-term passive investment strategy works best for most of us. As he says, "Very few people should be active investors."

It is humbling, but liberating, to give up trying to beat the market in favor of the Tao of just *being* the market. We can do this by buying a simple market index fund that replicates the performance of the stock market as a whole.

If you follow the financial press, you will occasionally come across stories debating the value of active versus passive management. This debate has been *over* for many years. It lingers in the commercial media only because so much money still rides on active management.

Minimize Expenses and Taxes

The index fund that diversifies our investments across the entire stock market does so for a fraction of what active management costs. Our annual expenses would be about 0.10 to 0.35 percent. No high-priced Wall Street talent is required here, because an index fund can be run by a ham sandwich. Miraculously, the same highly diversified investment with the low expenses also turns out to be extremely tax efficient, since the stock market as a whole doesn't turn over very often. By paying great attention to these small expenses, over time we will make a lot more money.

P.S.: Many brokerages advertise their extensive list of "no transaction fee" mutual funds, as if you are getting some kind of great deal here. All this means is that they have entered into a fee-sharing arrangement with the underlying mutual fund company. As a rule of thumb, any outside fund in one of these bazaars is going to have a high internal expense ratio that disqualifies it from serious consideration.

Buy and Hold Forever

There is a special level of Investment Hell reserved for people who try to time the market day by day. They are like weak antelope that are culled from the herd and eaten by jackals.

Here's how it works: When the market declines, market timers get worried and decide it would be a good idea to flee for the safety of cash or bonds, so they sell out. *Whew!* Dodged a bullet that time—as the market continues to sink on still more grim economic news.

Then, the market turns. No bell is wrung to summon them back in at the bottom. Suddenly, the market is up a thousand points. Another week and it is up another thousand points. The money honeys on CNBC are all laughing and scratching now. The market timers decide the crisis has passed and wade back in.

What's the problem? Effectively, they have just executed a gigantic sell-low-buy-high transaction. They have just destroyed years of long-term investment returns by following their gut feelings.

Even people who are smart enough to invest in an S&P 500 Index fund are not smart enough to buy and hold. From 1995 to 2005, their mistiming adventures meant they earned only 78 percent of what the index fund delivered over the total period.

At some point you will hear the idea that the world has changed and this time it's different: There is some New Order, New Paradigm, New Normal, New Economy. This is bunk. There is no new anything. There are just the same old financial products, repackaged.

~

**At some point you will hear the idea that this
time it's different: There is some New Order,
New Paradigm, New Normal, New Economy.
This is bunk. There is no new anything.**

Note: You can time the market over long periods, in
the sense that at some times that stock market is much
cheaper to buy than at others, and the lower your price at
the point of entry, the better your long-term returns are
likely to be. This is a subject for another book.

What's the Problem?

While this list of desirable investor behaviors is beautiful
in its transcendant purity, almost no one is constitution-
ally capable of following them in practice. Alas, as human
beings, investors are caught in a vice:

1. Investors are overconfident and overly fearful.
2. Investors hate losing money about twice as much
   as they like making money.

All that's necessary to crush them is:

3. Investors live in the here-and-now.

In a self-destructive cycle, investor overconfidence leads them to become performance-chasing whores, and then their hatred of loss causes them to bail when the market tanks. Investors have been advised to guard against this by knowing their "risk tolerance" and investing accordingly. But risk tolerance is a moving target. When people say they have a high risk tolerance, what they really mean is that they are willing to make a lot of money. Once the market goes down, their risk tolerance shrinks like an Italian suit in the washing machine.

When people say they have a high risk tolerance, what they really mean is that they are willing to make a lot of money.

We hoped that diversification would protect us from the big meltdown, but it didn't. It turns out that meaningful diversification is far harder to achieve than we thought.

Advisors usually recommend that, instead of owning one broad market index fund like the S&P 500, we further diversify by slicing-and-dicing the stock market into different segments, and then choosing a separate index fund to target each one. The result is the standard pie-chart portfolio (see Figure 4.1).

Figure 4.1 Everyone's Pie-Chart Portfolio

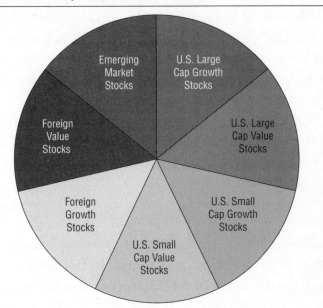

Look familiar? Almost all the stock portfolios out there in portfolioland are variations of this pie. You may own more or less of any of these segments, or you may add some sector fund like real estate investment trusts, or you may add commodities, but basically, this is it. If you got your portfolio out of a book, it probably looks a lot like this. In fact, if you *don't* own a portfolio like this, you may be doing something goofy and will be punished for it eventually.

Let us say that we bought this portfolio in January 1988. As of December 2008, our annualized return would have been 8.2 percent. This is slightly less than if we had just held the *total* U.S. stock market over the same period, which returned 8.8 percent. Our risks were actually *greater* in the more diversified portfolio.

What gives? It turns out that foreign stocks proved even riskier than U.S. stocks over this time period. Then, when everything fell apart, all these asset classes went into a tailspin at the same time.

If we are in a Boeing 777 cruising at 36,000 feet (or at *Dow 36,000* feet) and run out of gas, it really does not matter very much if we are sitting in the front of the plane or the back, or on the left side or the right. It does not matter if we are in the cockpit or the lavatory or the luggage compartment or we are standing on the wing. It is all going down together. Buying seven different tickets, or seven different asset classes, does not really buy us any more safety.

Many investors are victims of precisely this sort of *faux* diversification. They own many different mutual funds with misleadingly different-sounding names. The problem is that the funds all perform similarly, and never do they perform more similarly than when the market is cratering. What seems like protection turns out to be no protection at all when we really need it. Owning a basket of different equity asset classes does not save us.

The only significant diversification most people have comes from holding bonds or cash. This is partly because bonds have an enduringly low correlation to stocks, but mostly because (short-term, high-quality) bonds are themselves much lower in volatility. Once we know how much you own in the way of bonds (plus cash or money market funds), we can make a ballpark estimate as to how your portfolio is likely to perform. Your returns will be the returns of the market, squelched by however much you watered these down with bonds.

Table 4.1 shows this score box. It estimates historical returns based on every rolling 12-month period since 1926, adjusted for inflation, and shows the risks taken along the way to attain them.

If the portfolio is actively managed using stock picking or market timing, your results probably will not be this good. Additionally, Table 4.1 does not take account of management fees. These fees subtract directly from

Table 4.1   Everyman's Portfolio Performance Estimator

Stock/Bond Allocation	100/0	80/20	60/40	40/60	20/80	0/100
Average Annual Real Returns	8.4%	7.1%	5.9%	4.5%	3.2%	1.7%
Worst-Case Annual Loss	−64.0%	−54.0%	−42.0%	−28.0%	−18.8%	−15.9%

your annual returns and make your worst-case losses that much worse. If you are an index fund investor, your annual fees might be 0.25 percent. If you don't know what your fees are, and your account is at a large, name-brand Wall Street firm, your fees could be 10 times higher.

There's nothing particularly right or wrong with any of these portfolios. We might say, this is the external given. The problem is that almost no one buys and holds them—especially the ones that are equity-heavy. People do not buy and hold. They buy and sell. As the weak link in the chain, this turns all the other sound investing principles into so many useless good intentions. Even if we had been smart enough to wrest ourselves free from the Wall Street wealth-extraction machine by opting for index funds, and then had the iron discipline to hang on, we still anchored ourselves to market indexes that have lost half their value on two occasions during the past decade. No wonder investing isn't fun anymore.

**People do not buy and hold.
They buy and sell.**

Never fear, we will discuss this problem further in the next chapter and search for a way around it.

Additional Investing Do's and Don'ts

DO monitor your performance.

You know those thick brokerage statements you get in the mail every month or every quarter (well, they used to be thick, anyway)? They snow you with so much information that you have a devil of a time trying to figure out how your investments are doing.

All you really need to know is what your performance is compared with a similar portfolio of a matched set of index funds. If the brokerage firm is really clever, they will barrage you with indexes from all over the world, to make sure you are left scratching your head. They are betting that you won't want to look stupid by asking a simple question.

Go ahead and ask anyway. "How does my performance compare to a portfolio invested in a set of the most closely matched index funds?"

Here's another way you can find out: As a public service, and at enormous expense, your authors have put up a very simple calculator at www.tangentportfolio.com. Armed with your quarterly statement, you can take a stab at comparing your returns in a smackdown with a two-index-fund portfolio from Valley Forge, PA (Vanguard). This will just be a rough estimate, of course, but it is better than avoiding the subject entirely.

If your performance, over long periods, is significantly lagging the basic market indexes, this raises an interesting question: Should you drop your current program and invest in the index funds themselves?

DON'T use a *Cosmo*-style quiz to estimate your risk tolerance.

Brokerage firms love to give you these quizzes because the SEC makes them document that they really understand you. These questionnaires have no predictive validity, because there is no such thing as a generalized psychological trait of risk tolerance. Risk tolerance is contextually determined. However, feel free to use a *Cosmo*-style quiz to determine, "Is He Cheating on You? (the Rat!)."

Do's and Don'ts

- Do keep it simple and conservative, both with your portfolio and your individual investments within the portfolio.
- Don't assume that because you own a bunch of different-sounding mutual funds your investments are diversified.
- Do invest in passive index funds wherever possible.
- Do keep a close eye on fees, expenses, commissions, and taxes.
- Do buy and hold; don't buy and sell.
- Do monitor your investment performance.
- Don't use a *Cosmo*-style quiz to determine your risk tolerance.

Chapter Five

The Holy Grail
of Investing

*Having Your Cake and
Eating It, Too*

Now that we know how we *should not* invest, and how we *should* invest, and how we *actually* invest—where do we go from here? To start, let us introduce the Tangency Portfolio. The Tangency Portfolio is the Holy Grail of investing. It is the perfect investment—that ideal combination of everything (stocks, bonds, commodities, real estate, etc.) that gives you the highest return for the least amount of risk.

By analogy, you might say that once you have figured out that chocolate cake is the best desert in the world, you can have more chocolate cake or less chocolate cake, but nothing else will be better than chocolate cake. The same goes for the Tangency Portfolio. Once you have identified it, the only rational investment decision is how much of it you want to own. You can hold less by holding more cash alongside it, or you can hold more of it by borrowing money to lever up your stake. Either move will lower or raise your risk-adjusted returns better than any rearrangement of the holdings within the Tangency Portfolio itself. Any manipulations within the portfolio will only increase your risk more than they increase your returns.

It sounds pretty swell, doesn't it? So, wouldn't you like to know what the Tangency Portfolio is?

Well, we're not going to tell you. *Ha-ha,* just kidding. Okay, we'll tell you.

According to standard investment theory, the Tangency Portfolio is the portfolio of everything in the world. This is sometimes called the "market portfolio."

If you're rich, you may own a thick wedge of the global chocolate cake. If you're poor, you own only a very thin slice. However, to the extent that you are a rational economic agent, through thick or thin, your holdings will be diversified across all assets in the world as they are currently priced by the markets.

Next question: Where can we get our hands on this super-desirable portfolio?

It turns out: *nowhere*. There are thousands of mutual funds, yet no one offers a market-cap-weighted fund of all publicly traded global assets. Mutual fund companies are driven by marketing, not by economic theory. This is a shame, since it is not practical for each one of us separately to grab our checkbook and hop on a steamer, traveling around the world to buy a little bit of everything and have it shipped back to our casa.

The news isn't all bad, though. At least as far as stocks are concerned, one fund comes close: Vanguard's Total World Stock Index exchange-traded fund (ticker: VT). For 30 basis points (0.30 percent annually) it delivers the entire capitalization-weighted global stock portfolio to your door. Barclays' iShares All-Cap World Index Fund (ticker: ACWI) tracks the same index for five basis points more.

Is this the portfolio everyone should buy, then?

No. As we have discussed, investors lack the psychological stamina to hold onto their portfolios for long enough to reap the fabled long-term returns from the stock market. Their overconfidence leads them to jump aboard when the market is blasting off, but then they pull the ripcord when trouble comes.

Our response: Investors have approached investing backwards. Because losses are twice as salient as gains, we need to start with an acceptable predefined level of loss, and then reverse-engineer our portfolio with this loss already baked into the cake. The man/machine interface has to be redesigned to prevent the reckless investing mistakes that people predictably make.

Most portfolios start with Chicago Man, the utility-maximizing rational economic agent fervently believed in at the University of Chicago. We found Chicago Man and stood him on his head. Instead, we prepared a portfolio for the nut behind the wheel, the irrational Mr. Hyde who lurks within the breast of every investing Dr. Jekyll. Because if we don't start here, this slob is going to throw our investment returns under the bus first chance he gets.

We have to start not with Chicago Man, the utility-maximizing rational economic agent fervently believed in at the University of Chicago, but with the nut behind the wheel, the irrational Mr. Hyde who lurks within the breast of every investing Dr. Jekyll.

Here is the dilemma: If we add more stocks to get higher returns, we then jack up our risks and face even bigger losses in the next downturn. But if we saddle the portfolio with more bonds, we lower our returns and make it more likely we will jettison it during the next bubble. Therefore, we have to devise a portfolio that does well enough during both good times and bad times, so we have some hope of cashing in on the stocks-for-the-long-run returns we read about in books but which nobody seems to be able to locate on their brokerage statements.

This is another way of saying that we have to break— or at least stretch—the conventional risk/return barrier. Yet, how can we do better than with the market portfolio? How can we have our cake and eat it, too? To us, it seemed impossible.

The Fish in the Pond

Impossible, that is, until we read a 2004 paper by Olympian economists Eugene Fama (U. Chicago) and Ken French (Dartmouth), titled, "The Capital Asset Pricing Model: Theory and Evidence." Spelunking through the historical archives, Fama and French found that there were certain exploitable exceptions to the market portfolio's supremacy. What were these? They concluded that *"funds that concentrate on low beta stocks, small stocks, and value stocks will tend to produce positive abnormal returns . . . even when the fund managers have no special talent for picking winners"* (italics ours).

We stroked our beards as we thought about this. *Positive abnormal returns*—now that's the kind of abnormal we can relate to. *No special talent for picking winners*—again, it sounded like Fama and French were talking about us.

Let's dive deeper into their findings.

Within the stock market, stocks are always jumping around like fish in a pond. Every time the market makes a move, some stocks tend to jump even more. These are called *high-beta stocks* because they amplify the underlying volatility of the already-volatile stock market. However, there are also stocks, called *low-beta stocks* that do the opposite. The market can move a lot, but these fish are relatively quiescent. They mute the underlying variability of the stock market. These might be boring stocks like Consolidated Edison, General Mills, and Procter & Gamble. Fama and French were saying that the market underestimates stocks like these. That means they are mispriced—undervalued. That means their returns should be greater than expected. These types of companies offer market-like returns while displaying less volatility than the rest of the stock market. We'll take that deal any day.

The *small company stocks* might be like the little fish in the pond. A portfolio of skittish little fish certainly can be volatile. Big fish eat the little fish, or they die from natural causes, so many will perish. However, those that grow will produce outsize returns and more than make up for those who got an "F" in natural selection. No one can really tell which small fry are going to grow up to become whales, so we need to buy a whole basket of them. Fama and French were saying that, other things equal, this assortment should more than repay the additional risks.

Finally, Fama and French called out *value stocks*. A value stock is one that trades at a lower price relative to its economic fundamentals than its alternative, the growth stock. These might be likened to some of the older fish, since they seem to have no bright growth prospects ahead of them. AT&T, or Time Warner, or Dow Chemical would be examples. Fama and French were saying that if we own a whole bunch of these, the earnings surprises would likely come on the upside.

We turned these findings over in our fevered brains. Fama and French were two pretty big fish themselves, and their paper was a giant pink Valentine to investors. We figured we could use their findings to build a better asset allocation.

How Much Would You Like to Lose?

Then we had to tackle the dreaded issue of risk tolerance, a pitfall we discussed in the previous chapter. As bad times are inevitable, we knew that people had difficulty staying the course when their portfolios blew up in their faces like exploding cigars. Therefore, we would have to engineer portfolios that would lose a lot less than the conventional 60/40 (60 percent stocks/40 percent bonds) allocation would lose.

We turned to the historical record to see what the market had dished out in the way of big losses, to use as a benchmark. We factored in inflation. Who cares if a portfolio is up 10 percent one year if inflation is up 20 percent? We could go broke with returns like that. We adjusted everything so we were looking only at "real" (inflation-adjusted) historical returns. These were returns we could take to the grocery store.

Our starting point was the worst case a completely risk-averse investor would have faced from 1926 through 2009. This investor put all his money into 30-day T-bills. This is about as close to cash as we can get and still hope to have a slight upside.

What do you think this ultraconservative investor's portfolio returned during the worst 12-month period from 1926 to 2009, after inflation?

We were shocked and appalled to learn that, for the 12 months beginning April 1946, he lost 16.4 percent of his money. Here is this totally risk-averse guy, sitting in cash (although cash would have done worse, since—unlike

T-bills—cash pays no interest), and he lost one-sixth of his money that year. *Ouch*.

We then concocted three portfolios, each tailored according to how much an investor would be willing to lose in one of those really horrible, once-a-century years that seem to happen several times every hundred years. If the "risk-free" T-bill investor lost one-sixth of his money, we set up portfolios for people who would be willing to lose one-fifth of their money (down 20 percent), one-quarter of their money (down 25 percent), and one-third of their money (down 33.3 percent). We assumed that it would be very difficult for most people to lose more than a third of their financial assets in a year without jumping out the window, so we stopped there. To put these losses in perspective, an all-equity investor would have lost 64 percent of his money. Preparing for the worst we have experienced in the past century gives us a meaningful framework, since in that time markets have experienced wars, depression, recessions, deflation, inflation, and so on.

Unfortunately, there are no guarantees. Planning means preparing for events in proportion to their likelihood of occurrence. It is impossible to prepare for random, "black swan" events, since by definition they defy analysis. You might plan for a black swan only to be hit by a blue one. Things can always get worse. There might be nuclear wars, meteorites, global plagues, and so forth that make financial planning irrelevant. A portfolio can be bulletproof without being nuclear-bomb proof. There is no way to guarantee that even the most radical survivalist will be spared.

———————————— ∽ ————————————

It is impossible to plan for random, "black swan" events, since by definition they defy analysis. You might plan for a black swan only to be hit by a blue one.

The Tang Dynasty

Our alternative "how-much-are-you-willing-to-lose" portfolios relied on the Fama-French cheat sheet—low-beta stocks, small/value stocks, and government bonds would be the three slices of the pie. We would vary the size of each wedge depending on how much the investor was willing to risk losing along the way.

Unbelievably, no one offers an index fund of low-beta stocks. Most fund managers pick high beta stocks to try to beat the market when it is going up. This gets them on TV and racks up the short-term performance and star ratings to garner more assets from the lemmings who follow this nonsense. We wanted to do the opposite. This forced us to use four historically low-beta market sectors: Consumer Staples, Health Care, Utilities, and Energy.

Since "Consumer Staples" were not tracked as a separate asset class in the stock market database, we made our own index by combining all stocks from the food, candy, soda, beer, liquor, and tobacco groups. For "Health Care," we combined the stocks from the health services, medical equipment, and drugs and pharmaceutical groups. The Utility and Energy groups were used straight out of the box.

Then we used Fama and French's data series on *small company value stocks*, which kills two fish (small + value) with one stone. Since the low-beta stocks were less volatile than these, we used them in roughly a 1.5-to-1 proportion of low-beta to small/value stocks. Finally, on the fixed-income side, we topped off the portfolio with the same 5-year U.S. Treasury notes.

We called them the Tangent Portfolios^{SM}, as our own tweak on the marketwide Tangency Portfolio. The first portfolio is the "Tangent 20" since, historically, the most you would have lost holding it over any 12-month period from 1926 to 2009 after inflation was 20 percent of your initial stake. Then we built a Tangent 25 and a Tangent 33 using the same assets in different proportions, which would have lost 25 percent and 33 percent in the worst instance, respectively. The exact asset allocations that arrived at this happy conclusion are shown in Table 5.1.

Table 5.1   Tangent Portfolio Asset Allocation

Asset Class	Tangent 20	Tangent 25	Tangent 33
5-Year T-Notes	80%	60%	45%
Small/Value Stocks	8%	16%	22%
Consumer Staples	3%	6%	8%
Energy	3%	6%	8%
Utilities	3%	6%	8%
Health Care	3%	6%	8%

Table 5.2   Historical Portfolio Performance

Portfolio	Worst 12-Month Loss	Median Return
Indexed 20	−20%	3.3%
Tangent 20	−20%	3.8%
Indexed 25	−25%	4.0%
Tangent 25	−25%	5.6%
Indexed 33	−33%	4.7%
Tangent 33	−33%	7.1%

This all sounds very nice, but are these portfolios really any better than the plain-vanilla stock + bond portfolios? We constructed three benchmark portfolios that matched the same historical 1-year risk of loss as the Tangent Portfolios had, but this time composed from the Standard and Poor's composite stock index and the same 5-year U.S. Treasury notes. As Table 5.2 shows, in every case, the portfolios built from low-beta, small company, and value stocks gave us better returns at the same level of risk. The more equities we used, the higher

Figure 5.1   Tangent Portfolios Stretch the Risk/Return Barrier

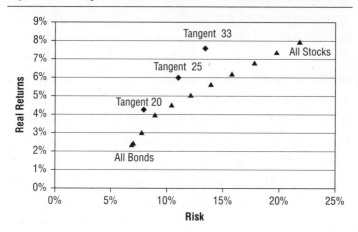

the margin of outperformance when compared to their benchmark stock + bond sisters, because these gave our stock sectors more elbow room to maneuver.

Based on the historical record from 1926 to 2008, we seem to have stretched the risk/return barrier. As shown in Figure 5.1, the Tangent 33 portfolio delivered nearly all of the returns of an all-stock portfolio at roughly half the level of risk.

What Does This Mean?

Let's translate statistics into dollars. What happened to an investor who put $10,000 into each of these portfolios, forgot about his money for 15 years, and then decided to open his brokerage statement and see how much money he had left after inflation? The results are shown in Table 5.3.

To put the historical worst-case scenarios in context, we also included the fifth percentile of cases. Here the odds are 1-in-20 against us. The last column shows the median (50th percentile) case. The median (50th percentile) case had us minting significant coinage. Naturally, the 50 percent of cases about the median did even better.

When Odysseus knew that he was going to be sailing past the Sirens—whose enchanting songs famously lured vessels to destruction on the rocks—he had his crew plug their ears with wax and lash him to the mast. Investors, knowing that hard times will come, need to make similar preparations. We need to decide in advance how much we are willing to lose and then lash ourselves to the plan. While no one knows what the future will bring, the Tangent Portfolios are a reasonable way to go in this regard, to the extent that the past hundred years are any guide.

Table 5.3 $10,000, 15-Year Performance, 1926–2009

Portfolio	Historical Worst Case	Historical 5th Percentile	Historical Median
Tangent 20	$ 9,150	$12,126	$16,376
Tangent 25	$10,864	$13,171	$21,753
Tangent 33	$12,028	$14,706	$26,588

Do's and Don'ts

- Do start by trying to plan for the worst scenario you are likely to face, since otherwise you will be tempted to scrap your investing program at the worst possible time and possibly destroy a lifetime of investing returns when you do.

- Do consider overweighting small company, value, and low-beta stocks in your portfolio to improve your overall risk-adjusted returns.

- Do check out the Tangent Portfolio website (www.tangent portfolio.com) for simple, doable, conservative portfolios that have stood the test of time.

Chapter Six

Bulletproofing Your Investments

~

A Recipe for Setting Up Your Tangent Portfolios

HERE IS THE SORT OF HEARTBREAKING e-mail that routinely lands in your authors' inbox:

> Dear Ben/Phil,
>
> If you guys think you're so smart then riddle me this. I took early retirement four years ago when American Widget downsized. Then Jess (my husband) got sick and we didn't have insurance and so we spent $37,234 on hospital bills that wiped out most of our savings, unfortunately.

Jess is okay now except his medicine costs $983.47 a month and all he does is stare out the window. Then again he never was the talkative type. Then Clementine (our cat) got leukemia and that cost another $1,500 and then she died anyway—can you believe it? But I still had about $90,000 in my IRA but now its worth more like $50,000(?) depending on which statement I read. It's not doing so good. With all my expenses it seems to go down about $5,000–$10,000 every month although I use coupons on Wednesdays. The good news is we own our house outright, which we bought for $250,000 in 2006. Our mortgage is $250,000 also. I was going to sell it to raise money but the realtor says wait. Meantime our new development is completely deserted except for these young hooligans using the house across the street at all hours plus I don't think they even own it! I called the police but nothing. Bill is a fine boy why did he have to hold up that liquor store? I bet Crystal put him up to it. That girl is trouble, trouble, trouble. So anyway there's only about $40,000 left but its going fast, and now it turns out I need a new head gasket and here they told me this used Jaguar was supposed to be a reliable car.

Can you recommend a good no-load mutual fund?

Polly

~

Our response:

Dear Polly,

Not only can we recommend a good mutual fund, we have a whole portfolio for you! Read on!

Sincerely,

Ben and Phil

It seems everyone wants to know how to set up an investment portfolio these days. Not just the theory, and not just the names of the specific investments—people want the basic steps to take them from the page to the stage. Of course, they could call any well-known brokerage firm, but that will triage them into the path of active management with the Wall Street wealth-transfer machine strapped onto their backs. How should a do-it-yourselfer proceed?

This chapter and the next cover the fundamentals of setting up and managing the Tangent Portfolios that we discussed in the previous chapter. We will shoehorn the beauty of the theoretical model into the available investment accounts and vehicles as best we can. The fit is not perfect, but it is good enough for home use. To make this a multimedia extravaganza, your authors have set up a website at www.tangentportfolio.com to make your investing life as simple as possible.

The Ingredients

Let's begin by running down the basic asset classes we need.

Bonds

To mimic the data in the previous chapter most closely, we would use a 5-year Treasury note to represent our bond allocation.

Of course, it's not that easy. If you buy a 5-year T-note today, in one year it has become a 4-year T-note, and in two years it's a 3-year T-note, and so on, so that won't work.

It's going to be easier just to buy an *exchange-traded fund (ETF)*. An ETF is simply a mutual fund in a tax-efficient wrapper that trades throughout the day like a stock. We like iShares Barclays' 3–7 Year Treasury Fund (ticker: IEI), which has an average duration of 4.4 years at a cost of 0.15 percent annually. Another choice would be Barclays' Intermediate Treasury Fund (ticker: ITE), which presently has a duration of 3.9 years. Either one should be dandy.

Even at this point, there's something to be said for U.S. Treasury securities. Notice how when the last crisis hit, they were suddenly what everybody in the world wanted to own. We want to anchor our portfolio in something that packs this much safety in terms of default risk. If you buy bonds from Belarus, you just don't sleep as soundly.

Notice how when a crisis hits, U.S. Treasuries are suddenly what everyone in the world wants to own.

Are there permissible variations here? Yes. For example, you might put half of the bond allocation in

Treasury inflation-protected bonds. Here we would choose iShares Barclays' TIPS Bond fund (ticker: TIP). The hope is that these bonds will work better in an inflationary environment. Nominal and inflation-protected Treasury bonds hedge each to some extent. We would especially recommend this course to retirees, who are the most vulnerable to inflation.

Many taxpayers prefer municipal bonds. Munis are perceived as being very safe, although this may turn out to be an accident of history rather than something divinely ordained. You can buy a national intermediate-term municipal bond fund in an exchange-traded fund wrapper: Market Vectors Intermediate Muni Fund (ticker: ITM). iShares S&P National Municipal Bond fund (ticker: MUB) is another one you might use, although it has a slightly longer duration. Our advice: Even if you love muni bonds, put half your bond allocation into U.S. government bonds and pay the taxes.

We are less crazy about corporate bonds and mortgage bonds. If you want to move down a bit in credit quality, Vanguard's Total U.S. bond market fund (ticker: BND) contains a little of everything (again, very Tangency-like).

We also recommend putting some of your bond allocation in foreign bonds. SPDR Barclays' International Treasury Bond fund is the vehicle we like here (ticker: BWX).

This fund buys treasury bonds from countries that you have heard of, so the credit quality should be okay. The thinking is: If the U.S. dollar declines, you will have a hedge. Many of the things you want to buy are made abroad and so you want to maintain your purchasing power. Having a global posture here is very Tangency-esque.

As for junk bonds or emerging market bonds: Do not go there. Be very afraid. Our goal with the bonds is to provide *stability*. For thrills we will look elsewhere.

Low-Beta Stocks

These again are boring companies that throw a wet blanket over the volatility of the stock market. Since there is no mutual fund specifically for low-beta stocks, we are going to use the sector funds corresponding to the ones we used in the previous chapter: Energy, Consumer Staples, Utilities, Health Care.

That part is straightforward enough. The next decision is: Do we want to use U.S.-only companies, or stocks from all over the world? We suggest the latter, because we want exposure to the global economy, and not just the U.S. economy. While the U.S. companies may be multinationals in many instances, it seems more Tangy to go all the way. The tradeoff is that the global funds are more expensive. The options are shown in Table 6.1.

Table 6.1   Low-Beta-Sector Funds

Sector	International	Expense	Domestic	Expense
Energy	IXC	0.48	XLE	0.21
Consumer Staples	KXI	0.48	XLP	0.21
Utilities	JXI	0.48	XLU	0.21
Health Care	IXJ	0.48	XLV	0.21

Small Value Stocks

Smaller value stocks have historically provided outsized returns, and these will form the third wedge in our portfolio pie. Dimensional Funds (DFA, www.dfaus.com), is the master of the small value stock territory, but you can access DFA funds only through a registered investment advisor. If you have enough in the way of assets to make that an option, this can be worthwhile.

If you are not going the investment-advisor route, worry not: You can still use exchange-traded funds in this space. Vanguard has the cheapest U.S. small company value fund. The companies in it are not quite as small or as deeply value as those in the DFA funds, which implies that its returns might not be quite as good, but they should still provide a respectable showing.

If you want international representation as well—which we highly recommend—you will have to pony up for some more expensive offerings. The foreign small-cap value fund we like best is from WisdomTree. We also

Table 6.2   Small/Value Funds

Region	Fund	Expense
U.S.	VBR	0.15
Foreign	DLS	0.58
Emerging Markets	DGS	0.63

are fans of Robert Arnott's foreign and emerging market funds (PDN and PXH, respectively). Our current recommendations are shown in Table 6.2.

All Together Now

Put them all together, and our reconstituted Tangent Portfolios, using exchange-traded funds, are shown in Table 6.3.

The three Tangent Portfolios are shown across the top of Table 6.3. The assorted asset classes that make up the portfolios are in the first column. To use the table:

1. Start by picking your maximum acceptable one-year loss (20 percent, 25 percent, or 33 percent), and then choose the Tangent Portfolio (Tangent 20, Tangent 25, or Tangent 33) that matches it.
2. Go down the column under that portfolio's name to find out what percentage of your investment assets to deploy into each fund.
3. Buy the appropriate exchange-traded fund (the tickers of each fund are displayed) in the proportions shown.

Table 6.3 Tangent Portfolio Allocations

Asset Class	Ticker	Tangent 20	Tangent 25	Tangent 33
Bonds				
Treasury	IEI	30%	25%	21%
Inflation	TIP	30%	25%	21%
Foreign	BWX	20%	10%	3%
Low-Beta Stocks				
Energy	IXC	3%	6%	8%
Consumer Staples	KXI	3%	6%	8%
Utilities	JXI	3%	6%	8%
Health Care	IXJ	3%	6%	8%
Small/Value Stocks				
U.S.	VBR	4%	8%	12%
Developed Markets	DLS	3%	5%	7%
Emerging Markets	DGS	1%	3%	4%
Total Expense Ratio		**0.29%**	**0.31%**	**0.33%**
% Non-Dollar Assets		**30%**	**30%**	**30%**

The last two rows give the annual fees to hold each portfolio for do-it-yourselfers along with the percentage of assets each portfolio holds that are not denominated in U.S. dollars. (*Hint:* It's 30 percent.)

To make your portfolio as easy as pie, we have set up a new website dedicated exclusively to this approach at www.tangentportfolio.com. There you will find a free space-age calculator that will let you enter any amount of money you want to invest in these portfolios and see a breakdown of the approximate number of shares to purchase of each fund—especially if it works.

But, before you go running to your computer to log on, remember the first step is deciding your maximum risk level. Here you will want to take into account your work situation. For example, if you are a Supreme Court Justice, you have a remarkable amount of job security compared to your sister the exotic dancer and photographer's model. Because your job is secure, you can afford to take much more risk with your investment portfolio. A recession or a depression is not going to affect you except to read about in the newspaper. You can afford the Tangent 33 portfolio, if not even more zing.

If you are a Supreme Court Justice, you have a remarkable amount of job security compared to your sister the exotic dancer and photographer's model.

Because we had made a few substitutions different from the Tangent model discussed in the previous chapter (adding foreign stocks, foreign bonds, and TIPs), we wondered if we might have inadvertently exposed investors to new dangers in the name of trying to make them safer. As a result, we looked at how these portfolios fared from November 2007 to November 2008, when the S&P 500 index fell 43.5 percent. During this period, foreign stocks fell even more than U.S. stocks, the dollar was appreciating, and inflation was negative, so all of our "improvements" worked against us. Fortunately, all the portfolios performed well within their tolerance limits during this catastrophic period for the rest of the market, thanks to their bond and low-beta stock holdings.

Do's and Don'ts

- Do assemble your portfolio based on how much you can stomach losing.

- Do make U.S. Treasury securities the centerfold of your fixed-income holdings. You don't want to have to worry about default risk the next time a crisis hits (unless that *is* the next crisis that hits).

- Do diversify globally with your stock and bond holdings.

- Don't forget to use inflation-protected bonds.

- Do take your career into account when deciding how much risk to take with your investments.

- Do use the calculator at www.tangentportfolio.com to estimate your initial purchases of the portfolio positions.

Chapter Seven

Pulling the Trigger

~

*Practicing Portfolio Management
at Home for Fun and Profit*

ONE DRAWBACK TO BEING a "do-it-yourselfer" when it comes to investing is that in many cases you actually have to do it yourself. No elves appear to magically do it for you. If you're married or have a boyfriend or girlfriend (or some combination), it's possible that your partner will do it all for you, but this convenience comes at the price of you not really knowing what's going on. Your ignorance might not turn out to be bliss.

Luckily, your diligent authors have detailed below all the steps necessary to invest for yourself. Pencils sharpened and blue books open? Okay, let's go.

Finding Mr. Right

It's all well and good to know exactly what securities you want to buy, but you can't just keep the mutual fund shares under your bed or in the garage. If you are a do-it-yourself investor, you first need an investment account at a brokerage firm. In fact, you may need more than one: an IRA and a taxable account as well.

Here's the rub: Our low-turnover, buy-and-hold mentality is exactly the opposite of what most Wall Street firms are looking for in a customer. They want someone who is going to be a trading machine, up day and night buying and selling stocks and generating commissions. You want to find a brokerage firm that will grudgingly take you on as a customer even though your use of their services is going to be minimalist. Fortunately, we've already done most of the digging for you.

Every year, *Barron's* ranks the best brokers, and in 2009, their favorite for long-term investors was Fidelity. *Barron's* also liked optionsXpress, Charles Schwab, TradeKing, Muriel Siebert, and E*Trade.

To compare:

- The **Fidelity Account** (www.fidelity.com) can be opened with $2,500, has no annual maintenance fees. It charges $19.95 for stock trades placed online (dropping to $10.95 per trade with over $50,000 in assets and to $8.95 with over $1 million in assets).
- **OptionsXpress** (www.optionsxpress.com) charges $14.95 per trade and has no minimum balance requirement. They do not charge extra for broker-assisted trades if you want to phone in your order. They also offer a practice account with play money to trade to learn how to place orders.
- **E*Trade** (www.etrade.com) charges $12.99 for stock trades in accounts with under $50,000 and $9.99 for accounts with over $50,000. There is an account inactivity fee of $40 per quarter for account balances under $10,000.
- **TradeKing** (www.tradeking.com) charges a super-low $4.95 for either an online or a phone-in (broker-assisted) stock trade. They have no account inactivity fees.
- **Muriel Siebert & Co.** (www.siebertnet.com) charges $14.95 for stock trades and has no account

maintenance or inactivity fees. There is a $30 fee for retirement accounts with balances under $10,000.

While not on the *Barron's* list, Vanguard (www .vanguard.com) is beloved by retail investors for its low-expense index mutual funds. However, its broker-age accounts are not competitive with those above unless you have substantial assets to custody with them. With $500,000, the commission schedule drops to $12 per trade (but starts at $40.50 for phone-in orders). At $1 million, the first 12 trades are free and $8 each thereafter.

This is a competitive marketplace and brokers and custodians are always shifting their cost structure to jockey for business, so perform your own due diligence and read the fine print before signing on. While fees matter, we are not going to be trading very often, so there is also the overall convenience to consider. These leads should be good places to start.

You Can Do It

Now that you are armed with a brokerage account(s), here's what you do to set up the Tangency Portfolio of your dreams:

1. Deposit your money into the brokerage account so it is funded.

2. Use the calculator at www.tangentportfolio.com to estimate how many shares of each fund to buy. If you are entering the trades online, you can look up a current price of the relevant exchange-traded fund by entering its ticker online. CNBC, bless their souls, offers free real-time price quotes on their website: www.cnbc.com. On most websites, quotes are 20 minutes old (as they are on our calculator, which gets its information from Yahoo! Finance).

3. Divide the price per share into the total amount you want to spend on that security. Since we cannot buy fractions of shares, we need to round them, and probably to round them down rather than up. While it is nice to buy 100- or 50-share lots, it is not essential.

4. Enter the trade into your broker's online trading system, or phone it in (for which there may be an extra charge for the extra handholding).

Once entered, the trade should execute almost instantly. Be careful when entering your last trade. You don't want to spend more money than you have left in the account. We hope the broker's website will not let you do this in any event. It's generally best to wait until the stock exchange has been open for an hour or so to make sure there is sufficient trading volume so that you can get the best execution on your order.

Tax Issues

Wait a minute—don't enter those trades yet. You have to figure out which securities to put in which type of account. Here our goal is to place the most tax-intensive securities in an IRA or 401(k) plan, to keep them from the grasping paws of the Internal Revenue Service. The good news is that the exchange-traded fund format is fairly tax efficient. Consult your own tax advisor for guidance on specifics. Do we look like accountants? (Don't answer that. . . .)

Since taxable bond funds pay taxable interest, these are excellent candidates for your IRA or 401(k). Inflation-protected bonds (TIPs) would go in first, since these can generate what is called "phantom income." This has nothing to do with the purple-clad cartoon crime fighter of yore. It refers to the IRS's practice of taxing you this year on interest from the bonds that will be paid only in the future. Next in line would be foreign bonds (BWX) and domestic treasuries (IEI).

Our preferences for what should go into tax-deferred accounts are shown in order in Table 7.1.

401(k) Plans

Question: How do we integrate the Tangent Portfolios with our 401(k) or 403(b) plans at work?

Answer: With difficulty.

Table 7.1   Funds to Put in Tax-Deferred Accounts (in Order of Preference)

TIP	Inflation-Protected Bonds
BWX	Foreign Bonds
IEI	Government Bonds
DGS	Emerging Market Stocks
DLS	Foreign Stocks
JXI	Utility Stocks
VBR	U.S. Small/Value Stocks
KXI	Consumer Staple Stocks
IXJ	Health-Care Stocks
IXC	Energy Stocks

The 401(k) plan has been an unmitigated disaster for American workers. Here's what we used to have: a defined-benefit plan, professionally managed, backed by a rudimentary government guarantee. This was something you could plan a retirement around. Here's what we swapped it for: a defined-contribution plan, self-managed (with demonstrably terrible results), high expenses, poor investment choices, and no guarantee of anything except chaos.

With no other alternatives, we have to do the best we can with the primitive tools we have been given. The first step we need to take is to dig into our statements and find out what our investment options are. The chances of finding the exact asset classes used in the Tangent Portfolios are nil. This means we have to make judicious substitutions.

The next step is to ferret out each fund's expense ratio. You will probably need a microscope to read it.

Neither your company nor the plan sponsor has any interest in letting employees know what a rotten deal they have cut on their behalf. If any fund has an expense ratio of more than 1 percent, simply cross it out. Otherwise, write down the expense ratio in the margins. Notice how the index funds have the lowest expense ratios.

Survey the candidates that are still standing. The first Tangent investment to squeeze into our 401(k) plan would be some kind of bond fund. These might be under a "Fixed Income" heading. The best we can hope for is a "U.S. Aggregate Bond Index" or "Total Bond Index" or "Government/Credit" bond fund. A "TIPS" or "Inflation-Protected" bond fund would be fine as well. Fit as much of your bond allocation as possible into this account.

At this point, you are leaving Tangentland. They will not have any sector funds in the area of Utilities, Health Care, Energy, or Consumer Staples. They are extremely unlikely to have any viable small company or value stock funds, either. If you have any headroom remaining after you have made your bond allocation, your only choice will probably be to use whatever generic S&P 500 Index fund (or Total Stock Market Index Fund) they offer.

If you are looking to limit downside risk with conventional index funds:

- For a 20 percent downside risk, use 24 percent S&P 500 and 76 percent bonds.

- For a 25 percent downside risk, use 36 percent S&P 500 and 64 percent bonds.
- For a 33 percent downside risk, use 47 percent S&P 500 and 53 percent bonds.

These portfolios should match the safety of the Tangent Portfolios, but they may not match the forward-looking returns, at least if history is our guide.

A final piece of advice: Whenever you leave your job, roll over your 401(k) plan into an IRA, where you will be able to choose from a vast library of low-cost investment options.

Adding and Withdrawing Funds

Now that your portfolio is set up, you can't just lie back in the hammock and watch TV. There is going to be occasional work to do. You may have to add more money from time to time, or take money out for living expenses.

When adding funds, the idea is to "top off" the portfolio. We calculate how much the portfolio will be worth with the new money added, and then multiply out the percentages from Table 6.3 and bring up each asset class as the math dictates. The calculator at www.tangentportfolio .com can help with this.

When drawing down the Tangent Portfolios, do the opposite. Calculate what the portfolio would be worth once the money is pulled out, enter that amount into the calculator, and then sell from the asset classes that are over their allotted dollar amount until you have extracted the cash you need. The guiding principle is to not sell any asset class that is unduly depressed by the economic climate of the moment. During bad times, we want to sell more from the bond side. Conversely, during a bull market, we sell more from the stock side.

This does not have to be an exact science. If we just add money to the one or two asset classes with the lowest value and withdraw money from the one or two asset classes with the highest value, that should be good enough.

This process is tantamount to rebalancing the portfolio on the fly. It is counterintuitive, because we are always buying what is doing the worst and selling what is doing the best. The motto is "Sell High, Buy Low"—an investment idea that has stood the test of time.

Rebalancing the Tangent Portfolios

Rebalancing is the same as adding and subtracting funds, except that we are not adding or withdrawing money—we are just rearranging the assets inside the accounts. Once again, the calculator at www.tangentportfolio.com shows us the correct allocation for our present asset value. We sell those asset classes that are over their specified amounts, and use the proceeds to buy shares in the other asset classes to bring them up to factory spec.

Rebalancing needs to be done only when the values of the asset classes have diverged meaningfully from the initial configuration. Under normal circumstances, every three years or so seems about right. In practice, you may need to rebalance only a few of the funds that are the most out of line.

Still Too Much?

If you don't want the job of running these portfolios yourself, www.tangentportfolio.com can refer you to an investment advisor who will implement these portfolios for you.

Now that you know how to invest, you need something to invest. That would be money. Where are you going to get it? We are going to devote the rest of the book to showing you.

Do's and Don'ts

- Do use a brokerage where fees are low and you won't be charged for infrequent trading.
- Do park assets where they will suffer the least at the hands of the taxman.
- Don't rebalance your portfolio just for its own sake. Wait until the underlying positions get significantly out of alignment. In normal circumstances, rebalancing once every three years is plenty.

Become the CEO
of You, Inc.

~

*Get Wise, Get Smart,
Get (Further) Educated*

As HARD AS IT IS TO INVEST SUCCESSFULLY, it is even harder to earn and save money.

Fortunately, you are chair and CEO of You, Inc.—the company that generates the income stream that fuels your life and will eventually power your retirement and your estate. It is worth paying enormous attention to this role, since—unless you are heir to a large fortune—it is the engine behind everything else. Much of your life will be devoted to transforming what economists call your human capital— your brains, your skills, your work habits, your winning personality and good looks—into financial capital. Our goal in this *Little Book* is to help you optimize this process.

Your education powers this advancement. What's this? You say you've already been to college and it's too late to redo the past? Not so; for one thing, you probably know some young people who could benefit from this advice. If these young people happen to be your children, then they especially need to hear it, since you want them to earn a lot of money to support you in your old age.

If you are in your forties or fifties, you may also have noticed that your income has plateaued. This is partly because your knowledge base has become stale. You might have experience but a young kid out of graduate school knows all the new stuff that's cool. He also works cheaper than you do and has a network of friends who will be remaking your business over the next decade. Instead of spending your spare time playing Windows Solitaire, you should go to every length to keep your education and contacts up-to-date, lest you cruise on autopilot into obsolescence.

Go to College, Get Some Knowledge

In an information-based, service economy, the simplest way to invest in your human capital is by acquiring an advanced education. We're spending less and less time working as field hands or down in the mines lately—have you noticed? Most Americans no longer rely on physical labor to bring home a paycheck. They go to school and acquire specialized training. Leveraging this investment of time and energy can yield a tremendous advantage that compounds over your entire lifetime.

As a university education has evolved from a privilege of social rank like dancing lessons to a perquisite of the middle-class lifestyle, college is now approached as a place for young people to spend four years experimenting with sex and alcohol and drugs while picking up a diploma before entering the real world. This prolonged adolescence is unfortunate because it underutilizes the tremendous opportunity that college represents. The goal here as everywhere should be to maximize utility, not squander it.

You might look at it this way. What is the competitive advantage that college offers? You have only a finite amount of time there. You might read *Pride and Prejudice*, or you might learn advanced statistics. What is the best use of your time on campus? Which book would be easier to crack once you are graduated?

Virtually any college degree is a ticket into the knowledge-worker economy. It supposedly shows the ability to sit in a chair, to understand verbal instructions, to analyze problems, to perform calculations and write at a basic level of competence, and to work on projects over time. People who spent college screwing off can still use that ticket to rise high in life by knuckling down once they hit in the labor force.

Yet, how much better off would we be if we used our time at college productively? What if, instead of four years of doing the minimum just to get by, we had taken the occasion to grow up and acquire self-discipline?

Majors for Minors

While all people are equal—black, white, Latino, Asian, gay, bisexual, and transgendered—not all college majors are equal in how much money their graduates earn. People who major in Engineering, Computer Science, Business, and Health professions earn significantly more money than those who major in Education, the Humanities, or in various "studies." It is no mystery why. Try *b.s.*-ing your way through an engineering exam and see how far you get.

Yet, colleges are now constituted so that it is possible to graduate without doing or learning much of anything. Nowhere is this truer than at elite Ivy League schools, where the various "studies" departments mean that you can leave school significantly more ignorant than when you entered. Think long and hard before majoring in French poetry or women's issues. If you're going to major in anthropology, you'd better be Indiana Jones. Otherwise, you are going to be entering a field where there are no jobs. You are going to have to do something else, which means starting over once you graduate. You will lose momentum.

Schools happily train students for exciting careers in fields where there are no jobs. Do not assume that just because an academic program is full that there is a job waiting at the other end. You need to investigate for yourself what the employment prospects are. You will learn more by blindly calling three people who work in the field and asking them than by spending a month at the career counseling office.

A fact that you might as well face right now is that careers that feel good usually don't pay well. If you are drawn to the psychology department or the religion department or the education department because the subject matter is so absorbing, be aware that it will likely launch you into a relatively low-paying job compared with where you might have landed had you applied the same industry somewhere else. You need to ask yourself: Would you rather work for a school, a hospital, or a welfare agency, or perhaps serve on the board of one?

Similarly, some students are drawn to political science in the hope of going to Washington and becoming "difference-makers." Our advice is to try this as a summer intern first. Working for the government will not pay you well unless you work at a high enough level to acquire important contacts.

In a culture of narcissism, it is not surprising that many overpraised children are drawn to the arts, where their instincts for self-expression come to full flowering. Unless your name is V. Van Gogh or W. A. Mozart, we cannot really recommend this path. In the real world, art is a ghetto of poverty and disillusionment. You may be a terrific pianist, but the most likely outcome of pursuing piano as a career is that 10 years from now you will be teaching small children how to play "Twinkle, Twinkle, Little Star" all day long, not tickling the ivories at Carnegie Hall.

If the things that come most easily are bad, what should you do instead? Do the things that are hard, of course. Take the hard courses—the ones cool kids want to avoid—and crack them like walnuts. This way, you will acquire the genuine self-esteem that comes from mastering difficult subjects. Remember how once mothers tried to guilt their kids into finishing their vegetables because of all the starving children in China? Well, now there are millions of super-smart Asian kids who eat hard subjects for breakfast. They are your future competition.

―――――――――――― ∽ ――――――――――――

Remember how once mothers tried to guilt their kids into finishing their vegetables because of all the starving children in China? Well, now there are millions of super-smart Asian kids who eat hard subjects for breakfast.

In other words—and this line of thinking is distinctly unfashionable, but once it would have been so obvious as to not need mentioning—we think college is best used as preparation for the real world, not as a four-year holiday. In the real world, people are not going to hire you because you are special and wonderful. Just being you gets you a job washing dishes. They will hire you because you have the specialized knowledge they need to solve a problem. College should be about acquiring essential and difficult skills for which there is demand in the marketplace and competition for the labor of those who ply them. At the undergraduate level, this generally means getting comfortable with calculus and statistics and the sciences. You should also learn to write well-organized expository prose. You should know your way around a computer. You should be able to make a clear and engaging presentation of your ideas to a group.

Higher Learning

The highest-paying career paths will involve going to graduate school. This will add to your expense but should be the best money you ever spend. Ideally, because you are a hard worker bee, you will go to a well-known and highly regarded graduate school that will make all future job searches that much easier. You will get a graduate degree in something genuinely useful like law or medicine (where the government restricts entry to the profession), business, engineering, or chemistry. With a professional degree, even if you decide to write novels like Michael Crichton, MD, did, you still have a career to fall back on as Plan B if your novel doesn't turn out to be *Jurassic Park*.

A word about the friends you make in college and graduate school: In your future life, almost every friendship you strike up through work—however great the guy or gal—will have something provisional about it. You might have to fire them, they might have to fire you, or you might be competing for the same slot. In any event, they eventually will be transferred to the Denver office and you'll rarely see them again. By comparison, the friends you acquire in school are golden and longer lasting than your work-related social buddies.

It can be a good idea to befriend your professors as well. It's rare for a professor to become friends with a student unless he's at the top of the class or (if the professor is a man and the student is a woman) she's a cutie-pie. If the professor likes you, his connections might be useful in getting you into a good graduate school or even a first job.

Finally, if there are any famous professors at your school, be sure and take their courses even if they are outside of your field. You will be able to dine out on these anecdotes for the rest of your life.

You, Inc. Do's and Don'ts

DO choose a direction early in life if you can.

The earlier you choose a direction, the better off you will be in that field. Of course there is a place for finding yourself and exploring what really turns you on. That place is called "high school." Most of us are not so prescient, though. There's nothing wrong with the classic liberal arts education, even if it is becoming rarer than the Abominable Snowman. You can always find your vocation in graduate school, assuming you fulfilled the entry requirements along the way. Nonetheless, a small change in a productive direction early in life can make a big difference to your lifetime standard of living, because its effect is amplified across decades.

A lot of life is a random walk. Many people spend years in young adulthood knocking around the pinball machine without ringing many bells or lighting many lights, until some lever finally launches them in a profitable direction. We all know people whose later careers bear scant relationship to their early education or training. Increasingly, people pack several different careers into a lifetime. We get this. The point remains that the sooner you know what you are going to do and the more hours you put in doing it, the more of an edge you will have over others.

DO be a builder.

School teaches you how to be a critic and tear things apart. That is great if you are going to get a job as a movie critic or a divorce lawyer. In the real world, success comes from building things. "The man who builds a factory builds a temple," Calvin Coolidge said. Critics and naysayers get pushed to the sidelines. A positive, cooperative, roll-up-your-sleeves attitude makes you someone who will contribute to the mainstream of progress. Do not lose sight of this.

DON'T waste time with losers.

If you hang out with people who are failures, losers, people with sad-sack, hard-luck stories, bad habits, bad attitudes, and serious problems, eventually you will feel right at home among them because you will have become one, too. We want to help people like this, but the way to do that is not by drinking beer and smoking cigarettes with them. Spend as much time as possible with people you want to be like. To get somewhere, hang out with the people who are already there.

DON'T do drugs or drink alcohol.

No, this is not an after-school special. The reality is that drugs and alcohol will destroy your human capital faster than anything else. Yet, college is seen as a time when it's okay to "experiment" with drugs. This is like "experimenting" with nitroglycerine. No experimentation is necessary because the outcome is known with certainty. If you start using drugs tomorrow the next couple of weeks will be fantastic. After that your life will be reduced to a cipher.

Life is undeniably difficult, and we all wish we had some easy way of escaping from the disappointments and anxieties it presents. The best way your authors have seen involves putting one foot in front of the other while maintaining faith in a Higher Power. Your mileage may vary.

Do's and Don'ts

- Do regard college as part of life, not a vacation.
- Do get as much education as you can, especially if it is in a field that leads to gainful employment.
- Do be a builder; don't be a critic.
- Don't hang out with anyone you don't want to become like.
- Don't indulge in drugs or alcohol except in homeopathic quantities.

Chapter Nine

Human Capital 411

~

Your Personal Human Potential Movement

ONCE YOU HAVE ACQUIRED AN EDUCATION, you have to sell your services in the marketplace. This is not as easy as it sounds.

Ideally, your career should be in that little sweet spot where three circles overlap: your passion, your talent, and the market. Or, the circles of what you love doing, what you are good at, and what people will pay for. If you score only two out of three, eventually you will run into trouble.

The most lucrative careers are in areas where there is a lot of money sloshing around. At the apogee, this would be: hedge fund manager or investment banker. It also applies to any field where you are working for rich people or close to a torrent of money. Even if you get just a lick off the Popsicle, if there's enough sugar, it can be very sweet. That's why Willy Sutton robbed banks: because that's where the money is. He didn't rob orphanages or libraries.

If you want to position yourself to become rich, work in a field where money aggregates. If there's not a lot of money there, you will not become rich, however fulfilling the work may be in other respects. It also helps to be in a field where people are completely dependent upon your services. The highest-paid careers are in areas like medicine, accounting, engineering, law, and management.

Sometimes people say that you shouldn't become a (lawyer/doctor/dentist/accountant/etc.) because there are already too many (lawyers/doctors/dentists/accountants/etc.) in your town. Economist Herbert Stein (Ben's father) provided the answer to this objection. He said that while indeed there may be a great many tax attorneys, there is always a shortage of really *good* tax attorneys. Anyone with 15 days' experience in the real world can tell you that excellence is in very short supply everywhere. If you can be the best at what you do, your supply will create its own demand. This is a high bar, however. You'd better be able to deliver.

If you can arrange to work for a person you admire and respect, this will enhance your life beyond measure. Remember that at least a quarter of the general population has a diagnosable mental illness. There are a lot of insane bosses out there, and working for one of these little Hitlers will make your life hell. It's not worth it.

And an important note: The world does not owe you a living. Work is a privilege. Work not only contributes to making the world a better place, it protects you from meaninglessness and insanity. People who don't work invariably fill their days with imaginary problems, the way lonely children fill their world with imaginary friends.

∿

People who don't work invariably fill their days with imaginary problems, the way lonely children fill their world with imaginary friends.

There's a Place

Where should you begin your career? You need to go to where the action is. For every heart's desire, there is some locale—some gaming table, as it were—where the game is being played. You can't win if you're not at the table, as the great Joan Didion said. If you want to be a surfer, you can't be in Peoria. If you want to act with the Royal Shakespeare Company, you can't do that in Spokane. If you are going into the country music business, you had better go to Nashville. Wherever it may be, you need to get to the "Nashville" of your business. The table will not come to you—you have to go to it. If you are at the table, paying your dues and keeping your eyes open for opportunities, eventually you will get to play.

You can't win if you're not at the table.

Every industry is different. As a general proposition, you are going to have to leave Smallville for the big, hairy city to maximize your career. Large cities open the possibility of Brownian movement and random Certs encounters that can spin your life into profitable and interesting new directions, personally as well as professionally. This is not likely to happen if you just see the same three people at Ma & Pa Kent's Country Store day after day. You won't draw the Opportunity Knocks cards you need to realize your potential. You will just get older and grayer with the passage of time, until one day you become Ma or Pa Kent yourself.

Sell Yourself

No matter what field you enter, your primary job is in sales. The ultimate product you are selling is you. You are selling yourself every day. The plastic surgeon? She's in sales. The interior decorator? Sales. President of the United States? Another sales job. Even though you may have leased your services to a large corporation, You, Inc. is in the business of selling you. We wish that every person in the United States could go through a basic sales training course. These people learn to be customer-centered, cheerful, helpful, problem-solvers. There is just no such thing as being too friendly or positive in your business persona.

As in sales, it will be necessary for you to develop a coating of rhinoceros hide to protect you from the criticism and rejection and low self-esteem engendered by the menial labor, long hours, and low pay you will have to endure when you start your career. There is no escaping these fraternity-hazing rituals.

At a minimum, you don't want to be an employee who subtracts utility from his or her company. Employees do this by being late or leaving early (a form of theft), wasting time, wasting the time of others, complaining—the usual stuff.

To get ahead, make yourself indispensable. Be known by the excellence of your work and your excellent work habits. You serve to conquer. Rule one is to make your boss look good. It goes without saying that he gets all the credit. Don't just take the blame, reach for it. This is the way of the world.

The important thing is to be an anti-entropic, value-adding, utility-maximizing employee. As long as you add demonstrable value to a profitable business, you will never be laid off. If you see that you are not adding more value than you cost for the company, you are in trouble and klaxon horns should be going off in your brain even if upper management hasn't noticed yet. Your days are numbered and you need to adjust.

You will never be successful in your dream career unless you work extremely hard at it. The idea that you will be discovered and arrive fully blown in your fantasy job is false. If you scratch beneath the surface of almost any story of personal accomplishment, you will find endless hours of people honing their craft.

To choose excellence is to choose a life of hard work. To choose a life spent doing something other than hard work is not to choose a life of excellence in your chosen field. There is no shame in this; it is the choice most of us make. Just don't expect to get the same results that workaholics do, professionally or monetarily.

Perception Becomes Reality

In the real world, first impressions are usually accurate. Neatness counts, spelling counts, grammar counts. Since no one can look into your soul, a first impression is as good a shot as you're ever likely to get.

Look at how successful people dress in your business, and then dress just like them. As Ben Franklin advised, dress to please others, not yourself. Manifestly, most people are terrible judges of what looks good on them. Here's a shortcut: Until our country institutes a badly needed national dress code, it is hard to go wrong buying all your clothes at Brooks Brothers.

Looking right for the part will take you a long way. Then you have to act right, too.

Just when it seems national standards of behavior cannot fall any further, they fall to record lows. Until a national etiquette police is empowered to issue citations, it is important to buck this trend.

Good manners have nothing to do with being formal or snooty, but simply with showing consideration for the feelings of others. The primary manners violation is people's endless self-obsession. Sometimes it seems like every person we meet is a broken radio capable of broadcasting but incapable of receiving. Like small babies who never got enough, these unfortunate people live in shallow pools of narcissism. Don't talk endlessly about yourself. Don't hijack the conversation at every opportunity to bring it back to you. There's enough oxygen on the planet for everyone.

In terms of basic manners, all the usual Emily Postings apply: Be on time. Send thank-you notes. Don't use profanity. Don't brag or show off. (It doesn't make people admire you; it makes people hate you.) Don't talk about politics or religion except to known converts. Talking about your diet or what you had for lunch isn't conversation; it's the opposite of conversation. Good manners by themselves won't get you ahead, but they will keep you from being shut out of future opportunities.

Investing in Your Human Capital Do's and Don'ts

DO have integrity and be a person of good character.

The single most important thing you can do to burnish your human capital is to be a person of good character. This means that you don't break the law, you tell the truth, you keep your word, and you take responsibility for your actions.

As Warren Buffett says, "We look for three things [in our managers]: intelligence, energy, and integrity. If they don't have the latter, then you should hope they don't have the first two either." Therefore, you have to protect your reputation. It takes only one stupid decision to ruin it. Like fine China, your reputation can be repaired, but it loses most of its value once cracked and is never really the same again.

DON'T count on life being fair.

Fairness is like a rainbow: beautiful when you see it, but rarely occurring. Insisting on fairness is a recipe for misery. Some people go around measuring everything with a mental yardstick of fairness and conclude they are always getting the short end of the stick. Of course, these people are not comparing themselves to the guy who's twice as smart as they are but who spends his life stooped in a rice paddy in a North Korean forced-labor camp.

DO live in the real world.

The politically correct cocoon of college campus is poor preparation for the world outside. The sooner you eject that baggage, the happier you will be. In short:

- *Lookism exists.* People who are good looking are assumed to have other positive characteristics that they may not possess in reality. People love being around good-looking people. This is a fact—not fair, but a fact.
- *Sexism exists.* Men do better than women, primarily because they do not move in and out of the workforce to raise babies. Women may be better at what they do, but seniority is a real factor and if you lose it, there are consequences.

- *Ageism exists.* Being older is a significant drawback in almost every field.
- *Nepotism/favoritism exists.* Whom you know matters more than what you know. Again, this is not fair, but it is usually true. People want to do business with people they like, which is to say, people want to do business with people like them, or at least superficially like them.

DO use your time wisely—it's a wasting asset.

Rich and poor people are equal in one important respect: They're both given 24 hours to spend every day. If you spend all your free time in the La-Z-Boy watching TV or at yoga class or a sports bar or the Cineplex, it will add little to your bottom line. If you spend lots of time at the gym or Starbucks or in Internet chat rooms or online gaming communities, you are unconsciously making a consequential choice about your lifetime standard of living. In other words, you'll pay for it.

In fact, you need to ask how much "free" time you really have. Most jobs that are going to make you the success that you want to be simply do not have quitting times. If you could be spending your time building your human capital by studying or by staying abreast in the latest developments in your field or just responding to client e-mails, that will do you more good than watching *American Idol*.

DO read the *Wall Street Journal* every morning.

Sure, there are dozens of highly successful people in the United States who do not—hundreds, probably. But are you likely to become one of them? Our friend Ron Harkey gives a talk to corporate audiences called, "How to Read the *Wall Street Journal* in Only 7 Minutes—Impossible! Yet It Must Be Done." That is the recommended primer here. Read the *Journal* every morning unless you want to end up like one of those unemployed guys you see playing chess all day in the park.

Sure, there are dozens of highly successful people in the United States who do not read the *Wall Street Journal* every morning. But are you likely to become one of them?

DO marry a sensible person.

When it comes to allocating the scarce resource of love, a long-term investment will prove the most rewarding. Day traders will have a few good hits here and there but in the context of years of quiet desperation. High-quality bonds yield more than junk, after accounting for the high default rate among the latter. Junk situations can look superficially appealing, but the sooner you exit these positions, the better off you will be.

If you are going to get anything out of a relationship, you need to be fully invested. This assumes reciprocity and a monopoly. If, after a brief while, you still have to compete with others, sell the entire position at a loss and move to the sidelines until a better opportunity appears.

Given the law of large numbers, given world enough and time, there *is* someone who has looks like Charlize Theron or Tom Cruise who has millions of dollars who would be willing to marry you. The problem is, you may be dead before you find this person. You will also encounter a great deal of rejection along the way from millionaire movie-star lookalikes who unfortunately do *not* want to marry you. At some point, the search process needs to close.

Over time, the returns on your investment should roughly equal the cost. What you put in by way of unselfishness, kindness, and patience should be repaid. If this is not the case, then you either failed to perform due diligence, your forecasts were unrealistic, or both.

Divorce is a swamp. While a divorce may be necessary for your mental health, it is very costly in terms of time and dollars and emotional energy. Preferably, your spouse will be supportive of your career and will not be a huge drain on your pocketbook with his or her expensive taste and free-spending habits. You do not want to marry someone who is high maintenance, either financially or emotionally (and they often go together), as intriguing as such a person might appear initially.

When you are in courtship, you are seeing the other person at his or her best. What you see will not improve after you marry; it will get worse. Do not fantasize for one moment that you will be able to "change" anyone. However, if you are able to overlook your own considerable shortcomings, it is possible that you can overlook those of your intended. The good news is that if you marry right basically your life will be right.

DO keep in mind that children are expensive.

After school busing destroyed the pubic school system, many parents must now work two jobs to send their children to private schools. The admissions ordeal (which begins with coaching to get your kid into the right competitive preschool) and tuition checks are but an aperitif. The modern parent has to open a vein for every kind of lesson, ballet, horse, music, math tutoring, and club on campus. Hours will be spent standing in the hot sun watching soccer practice that would try the patience of Mahatma Gandhi; endless chauffeuring to "play dates";

school fundraising and capital campaigns; enforced social engagements with the parents of Junior's classmates. Then, should Missy deviate from the norm in any respect, a platoon of self-dealing and cross-referring child therapists take control of your lives.

All this is prologue to the Darwinian struggle to get into Olde Ivy—a campaign that would give Erwin Rommel pause. Enter the educational consultants, tutors for the college boards, nightmarish family trips to remote college burgs, and the clocking of "community service" hours (preferably in Zimbabwe) for the college resume to show how much your Little Fauntleroy—who in real life swings cats by the tail—really cares.

The final laugh occurs when the daughter with the half-million-dollar education gets a job as a masseuse, and the son with the MBA cannot get a job at all, moves back home, smokes reefer, and practices drums all night.

The final laugh comes when the daughter with the half-million-dollar education gets a job as a masseuse.

While your authors take tremendous joy in their own children, we regretfully observe that our experience is far from universal.

Do's and Don'ts

- Do be a person of good character and earn the trust that others place in you.

- Do pay attention to appearances and mind your manners; first impressions count.

- Do remember that an attitude of gratitude is the surest get-rich-quick scheme.

- Do get over the fact that life isn't fair and start living in the real world.

- Don't waste your—or other people's—time.

- Do read the *Wall Street Journal* every morning.

- Do marry and stay married to a sensible person, especially if you can find one.

- Do keep in mind that children today are luxury goods.

Chapter Ten

Save 'Til You Drop

~

Topping off Your Piggy Bank

Do you enjoy worrying about money? Lying in bed in the middle of the night, listening to the faucet drip, wondering where the money will come from to pay that big tax bill, cover that tuition check, meet that mortgage payment, keep American Express at bay? It seems like your authors spend an inordinate amount of time dwelling on such matters, when our minds should be devoted to philosophy and the fine arts. Looking back, it's easy to see how all this endless worry and anxiety about money might have been avoided, had we only been as smart as you are about to be.

Creating a low-profile, low-maintenance, low-overhead lifestyle is the key to a refreshing night's sleep. Yes, even in a crazy, gotta-have-a-gimmick world turbocharged by credit cards, you should not spend every dollar that comes your way. Charles Dickens expressed it succinctly in *David Copperfield*: "Annual income twenty pounds, annual expenditure nineteen and six, result happiness. Annual income twenty pounds, annual expenditure twenty pounds ought and six, result misery." This is a fundamental difference between people, and it becomes obvious who is whom once a recession hits. Those who live below their means continue with their lives. Those who don't have to dissolve their lives in order to pay back creditors.

Warren Buffett still lives in the same stucco house he bought in 1957 for $31,500. His sidekick, Charlie Munger, didn't splurge by buying a new car until he was in his fifties, by which time he was a billionaire. In fact, when Charlie was single, he deliberately drove a beater to keep the gold diggers away. Note that the amount of money you save by buying a reliable used car and keeping it for a long time versus continuously leasing the latest model will be enough to pay for a new kidney when you need one.

Yet, something odd has happened over the course of our lifetimes. There has been a subtle (or maybe not-so-subtle) shift in public opinion. In the postwar era, a person was not what he or she owned. Some people were rich and others were poor and many others were in-between, but a person's worth was not measured by the sum total of his or her possessions. Madison Avenue has changed this. Now it feels necessary to own the latest and most expensive not just of a few things but of everything. Otherwise, we are life's losers. Even middle-class people today have anxieties that they don't live like movie stars. All this is false. You are *not* what you own—which in the end is mostly a bunch of junk—and neither is anyone else.

Small Is Beautiful

As difficult as the "buy and hold" is on the investing side, so is the "saving" on the accumulation side. If we are prudent, we will not take all the money we earn today and spend it on our present selves. We have to forgo owning many things we would like—toys, cars, vacations, furniture, art, jewelry, clothes—and save the money instead for our future old, frail, and ill selves. If you are like most Americans, it will scarcely be possible for you to save enough.

This again points to the need for a financial plan to guide your journey. Without one, you will be adrift at sea.

Your getting and spending will be regulated only by how much money you have in your wallet, how much headroom (if any) you have left on your credit cards, and how many things you want to buy (potentially limitless).

If you just look at how much you have left over at the end of every month, you will probably never save anything unless you have a high-paying job. The only thing that seems to work for most people is to automate the savings process. For instance, this happens when the bank directly deducts our mortgage payment and when we fund our 401(k) plans from our paycheck. What we should add to this is an automatic monthly transfer into a brokerage account (probably at Vanguard or Fidelity), where the money will be used to buy (at no commission) some index mutual funds from their lineup. If we don't make saving a high priority, the likelihood is that it will never happen.

In theory, there are two possible errors here: saving too much money, or not saving enough. But these two outcomes are not evenly balanced. Saving too much money leads to a sense of nostalgic regret from a rocking chair in front of a crackling fire with a dog at your feet and a snifter of brandy by your side. Not saving enough money leads to pushing a shopping cart holding all your possessions down a wintry street and sleeping in doorways. Since the contingency of being old, sick, defenseless, and poor is too horrible even to imagine, and with so many indeterminates lying between here and our old age, everything dictates that we err on the side of oversaving today.

Since the contingency of being old, sick, defenseless, and poor is too horrible even to imagine, everything dictates that we err on the side of oversaving.

Become Well Insured

Insurance is your first line of defense when it comes to defending your assets. The cheapest form of insurance is self-insurance, out of your own vast savings. However, you probably can't afford it.

Yes, you need home insurance or renter's insurance, flood insurance, disability insurance, long-term care insurance, life insurance, auto insurance, health insurance, and an umbrella policy covering anything that is left over. Depending on your situation, you may need other types of insurance as well. It is surprising how many people will purchase an insurance policy on a $39 clock radio from Best Buy, but fail to buy disability insurance, which might actually save their families.

In our previous tomes, we have sung the praises of term life insurance as the best low-cost option for many people. Let us pause here to say a few words on behalf of whole life. A whole life policy, bought with a careful eye on expenses, can be a friend in time of need. In a financial crisis like 2008, if you needed liquidity when all your other assets were beaten down, you could have borrowed tax-free against your whole life policy and used the money to pay for anything that needed paying: a new roof, the mortgage, an operation, or to simply tide you over until you found a new job. If you had died in 2008 (perhaps of a sudden heart attack after reading your brokerage statements), the value of your whole life policy would have been there for your survivors at a time when not much else was present and accounted for. It's worth considering.

The point of insurance is to pool risk and protect you from calamity. We also want to call special attention to your umbrella policy. When people decide that you have done them wrong and want to sue you within an inch of your life, they cannot sue you directly. They need to hire an attorney. However, the attorney's interests do not align perfectly with theirs. Insurance gives you the opportunity to drive a wedge between the two.

The attorney has no emotional agenda against you. Like anyone else, he wants to make as much money as possible for doing as little work as possible. If you can dangle a tidy sum of insurance money within his easy reach, this creates a favorable psychology toward a quick settlement. Their attorney suddenly will become your advocate, pressing your opponents to settle and move on with their lives. For the suit to drag on it is going to take a lot of his time and resources, and the amount of the final payout will be uncertain and may prove difficult to collect no matter what the judgment is. Against this prospect, any attorney will want to take the money on the table and run. You need enough insurance to make this outcome likely.

Cover Your Assets

By the way, if you are in a position where you might be sued—which is to say, if you have significant assets—or if you might find yourself facing bankruptcy (more common than divorce these days), you should give some thought to asset protection. Ideally, you will do this years before such contingencies arise, so you cannot be accused of "fraud in the conveyance" and risk having a judge undo the protections you have set in place. While this subject needs to be addressed with an attorney, here are a few examples:

- **Retirement accounts** generally are well protected. ERISA accounts, like 401(k)s, are yours to keep, as is the first $1,000,000 in IRA accounts (this may vary from state to state). A lawsuit might take you to the cleaners, but these accounts should be left standing, as O.J. was pleased to discover.

- States typically offer some exemption on the equity in your **homestead**. This amount has now been capped at $125,000, and in most states it is less. You may have to file a homestead declaration with your state in order to secure this protection.

- **Insurance products and annuities** typically are protected from creditors, but this protection also varies greatly from state to state.

- If you are starting a business, you almost certainly will want to do so using a **limited liability company** or some structure that protects your personal assets from attachment by creditors.

Families concerned with asset protection are often advised to separate their "safe" assets (personal residence, business interests, investment accounts) from their "risky assets" (cars, boats, rental properties) and place each into *Family Limited Partnerships or Limited Liability Companies* so that problems with the risky assets do not easily reach the safe assets.

Finally, your dog is your greatest asset. Protect him or her with all your might.

Getting and Spending Do's and Don'ts

DON'T shop to stave off loneliness or to purchase self-esteem.

Adam Smith observed that the chief enjoyment of riches consists in the parade of riches. At the extreme, you have your high school girls with their fake Louis Vuitton purses. Everyone we see shopping in Beverly Hills seems like these high schools girls, now grown up, but still play acting that they are rich.

DON'T bank on that big future payoff.

This is standard practice in Hollywood. Some big pay-off is coming in the future when you become a star that will magically solve all your problems and can be used to underwrite an opulent lifestyle in the meantime. We do not deserve more than we have right now. The big life-changing payoff rarely comes.

DO have a reserve fund.

In the event you find yourself out of a job, you need enough cash to tide the family unit over until you are employed once more. When you lose your job, within two weeks the transmission will fall out of your car, your house will need a new roof, and you'll have to fly back to New Zealand to visit your dad in the hospital. Your cash reserve fund should be enough to cover these kinds of contingencies, because when you are laid off it will likely be in the middle of an economic downturn and you won't want to sell your stocks when they are beaten down.

As a general rule of thumb, you need somewhere between three months' to one year's worth of living expenses in your reserve fund, but how much depends on what a hot property you are in the job marketplace. If you work on the Chrysler assembly line, save more. If you work for the IRS, you may scarcely need a reserve fund at all. We rarely hear people complaining that they have too much ready cash on hand when trouble arises.

DO pay your taxes.

Unbelievably, some people like to play games with their taxes, shaving a little bit here, conveniently forgetting about that income there, overstating deductions, and so on. This is suicidal. The taxing authorities have the kind of limitless power over you that Stalin would have envied. If you want to invite years of needless misery into your life, play cutesy with your tax returns. This holds true even if the Secretary of the Treasury himself is a tax cheat.

Don't think that you can cleverly avoid paying taxes by moving money to an offshore account. Here is a secret: There are no such things as secrets. Somebody always knows, and everything comes out eventually. This is as true in your financial life as it is in your sex life. For most people, the only benefit to such an account would be if they were to decide to leave the United States permanently. This is not worth planning for unless you are an organized crime kingpin.

DON'T borrow money, except to buy an appreciating asset.

That is, something that is going to go up in value over time. Education is ordinarily an appreciating asset and a terrific investment. By way of contrast, if one wanted to find the exact opposite of an appreciating asset, it would be travel. Travel is a wasting asset whose value vanishes the moment you step off the tarmac. With regard to your investments, we are not crazy about going on margin for your stock portfolio, because it supercharges the volatility and leaves you open to losing everything. Losing 30 or 40 percent is bad enough; losing everything starts to look like real carelessness. If you have ever been on the receiving end of a margin call from your broker, you know it is not a hugely enjoyable experience.

Credit cards are invariably used to buy instantly depreciating assets like food and clothing. They are Kryptonite and should be handled accordingly. If you run a balance on your credit cards from month to month, you should not have credit cards, period. Pay off the balance ASAP and use debit cards instead, unless you enjoy being a slave to a bank. For most people, credit cards are like cigarettes: a slow way to commit (financial) suicide.

The ultimate depreciating asset is a loan to a friend. Don't borrow from (or lend to) friends or family unless the money is needed to pay for a life-saving operation for an only child. As the adage says, you will lose both the friend and the money. If you must a borrower or a lender be, there is a website called Virgin Money (www .virginmoneyus.com) that, for a fee, will formalize the loan process and perhaps make the arrangement work less disastrously than it always does in such cases.

Do's and Don'ts

- Do live below your means.
- Do save 'til you drop.
- Do what you can to protect your assets from creditors, lawsuits, and evil ex-spouses.
- Do have a reserve fund.
- Don't play games with the IRS.
- Don't borrow money except to buy an appreciating asset.

Chapter Eleven

Houses of Blues

—————— ~ ——————

Welcome to the Neighborhood of Poverty

YOUR HUMBLE AUTHOR BEN STEIN was once considering buying a house on the Eastern Shore in Virginia. He decided to run the prospect past his pop, economist Herbert Stein:

Herbert: "Can you afford it?"
Ben: "I think I can buy it without putting myself in the neighborhood of poverty."

Herbert: "That's good, because that's a neighborhood you never want to be near."

Ben didn't buy the house.

~

Our home is usually our single most significant asset. Yet the whole subject of housing is nettlesome, especially now that the value of residential real estate has fallen off the map, and is only beginning to claw its way back. Real estate was touted as the "safe" investment after the tech debacle of early 2000 through 2002, but something has gone very, very wrong. Houses became the subject of a speculative bubble and then the bursting of that bubble. First, our stock portfolios were wiped out, and then our houses (yes, even with the new Sub-Zero refrigerators and Viking stoves) were, too. Like everything else, the benefits of houses can be (and were) oversold.

If only we had listened to Ben's dad. . . .

Let's Cut to the Finish Line

Do buy your house. While it will turn into an investment over time, you should buy it as a place to live. The reason why housing is desirable as an investment is obscure: It is because when you own your home, in effect you pay the rent to yourself, but you don't have to pay tax on that (implied) rental income. The economic desirability of homeownership is primarily a byproduct of the tax code.

───────────── ∼ ─────────────

The economic desirability of homeownership is primarily a byproduct of the tax code.

───────────────────────────────

Get it? Imagine that you and your neighbor have identical homes in a subdivision. Instead of your owning the house you live in and his owning the house he lives in, you own his house and he owns your house. At the end of every month, he writes a rent check to you and you write an identical rent check to him. At this point, Uncle Sam reaches into both your pockets and taxes the rent as income. However, when you and your neighbor each own your own house, your living situation is unchanged, but Uncle Sam leaves you alone. This is not true in every country. It is one way the government subsidizes residential real estate in the United States, and you should take advantage of it.

There are other government subsidies as well. Realtors always talk about the mortgage tax deduction—the fact that your mortgage interest can be deducted from your taxable income. However, people who don't claim this deduction can still take the standard deduction, which is around $9,500, so the true mortgage deduction benefit for middle-income people is the annual amount of mortgage interest less $9,500, not the absolute amount of the mortgage interest versus no deduction at all. Since the mortgage interest lowers every year on an amortization schedule, a crossover will come in the life of every mortgage when the standard deduction will be worth more.

The government subsidizes the mortgage interest rate on home loans up to a certain size. These are the so-called "conforming" loans bought by Fannie Mae and Freddie Mac. The government will also overlook the first $250,000 of capital gains ($500,000 for couples) when you sell your house.

The government affects the finances of home buying indirectly as well. Elementary and high school education are government monopolies paid for by your property taxes. If you plan to have children, you will be better off living in an area with a non-dysfunctional school system, if you can still find one (good luck!). This will eliminate the line item of private school tuition from your family's budget. The more children you have, the better a deal this is. A good public school system is an insurance policy protecting the value of your home.

Apart from the government subsidies, a strong economic case can still be made for homeownership. Since most people cannot afford to pay cash for a house, they have to borrow money to buy one, so the home becomes a leveraged investment. For the price of 20 percent down, they get exposure to 100 percent of the house's value in the marketplace. Most of the time in most places, home price appreciation after inflation has been small according to Yale's Professor Robert Shiller: perhaps 0.4 percent per year. Long-term owners can find that they have almost doubled their money after inflation. In addition, the imputed rent gives you an annual return of about 6 to 8 percent, inflation-adjusted and tax-free. Homeownership amounts to a stealth form of enforced savings. Lenders take away people's houses when the owners fail to pay their mortgages. Since people generally have equity in their homes that they do not want to lose, paying the mortgage becomes a marked priority. Even when they see a pretty new hat in the window at Bloomingdales, they pass on it and pay the mortgage instead. After 30 years of this monthly discipline, it turns out they own a significant asset.

Is Your House a Financial Asset?

People sometimes ponder whether a house should be considered an asset or an item of consumption. The answer mostly depends on the time scale and partly on your location. In the short run, a house is for consumption. If you have to sell it in a down market after having bought at the top, as many people are now doing, it will prove devastatingly expensive. If you hang in for the long haul, what was an item of consumption is alchemically transmuted into a major asset. It's true that you have to live somewhere, but after 30 years you may be ready to downsize to a smaller house, or move to a lower-cost area, or even to rent. Renting during retirement lets you remove the house from your estate and transfer the money into current consumption, where it may be badly needed.

Real estate markets are local. On the coasts where palm trees grow, they are far more prone to a boom-and-bust cycle than Shiller's steady 0.4 percent increase that prevails in Minnesota or Arkansas. In hot markets, your returns will depend on your entry point. Buy during a crash, and your long-term returns should be handsome. Buy near the peak, when people are snatching up trophy properties for their trophy wives, and you may wait a long time before you see a positive return.

Regardless, real estate is a real asset, which means that it is protected from the ravages of inflation. This is another economic benefit of homeownership. If, heaven forfend, our country experiences another round of 1970s-style inflation, or worse, your home—and that portion of your net worth—should be protected (but there are no guarantees).

Even if there were no economic benefits whatever to homeownership, there are such significant psychological benefits that many people would do so anyway. It frees you from the insanity of dealing with landlords. You can decorate it however you want. You can pound nails into the walls. You can make your home an extension of your personality, for good or for evil. This gives you a sense of control and peace of mind.

According to the Federal Reserve's Survey of Consumer Finances, homeowners as a group are significantly richer than non-homeowners are, even when controlling for the usual suspects like age, gender, race, employment status, and so forth. In addition to the equity in their homes, homeowners have significantly more money in investment accounts, IRAs, 401(k)s, and so on. Perhaps renters never put down the kind of roots that are usually required to amass wealth. Perhaps homeowners as a group are more disciplined. Perhaps they just fit in better with the stream of things and so get ahead. There are undoubtedly many exceptions. Unfortunately, this does not mean that you can just give someone a cheap loan to buy a house and that will automatically make him rich, as we learned during the ongoing property collapse.

Housing Do's and Don'ts

DON'T own your home.

That is, not if you are young and just starting out in your career. It is far more important to advance in your work than it is to own a house. You don't want the home to be an anchor holding you back.

You also will want to pass on the opportunity if you are single and might marry someone who might not want to live in your home, or if there's any reason why you are likely to have to move within five years. Renting frees up money for current consumption that would otherwise be tied up in home equity.

DO start saving for your down payment as soon as you can.

If you fit the home-owning profile, this should take priority over almost every other expenditure, on a par with your retirement savings, since essentially it is a form of retirement savings.

DON'T overpay for your home.

Don't buy your home in the middle of the real estate equivalent of Shark Week on the Discovery Channel. When houses are selling with multiple offers over listing price within days of being listed, it's time to chill. Wait a couple of years and buy them after the crash.

DON'T make yourself "house-poor."

You are house poor when your house owns you instead of the other way around. Remember that many of the expenses of owning a home are relentless, and the money tied up in the property is illiquid. Unless you have a comfortable margin of safety that allows you to put food on the table, you will sleep better if you rent.

DON'T take on a mortgage at a low "teaser" rate that resets to some higher rate later.

When it comes to mortgages, as with all financial products, the less gimmicky, the better. You can count on any change in your mortgage rate later coming at exactly the wrong time and working against you. Don't assume for a moment that you will be able to roll your mortgage over, either. If you can't afford a house with (preferably) 20 percent down and a plain-vanilla, 30-year fixed-rate mortgage, you can't afford the house.

DO avoid redecorating insofar as possible.

Once you are in the position of having to remodel or redecorate, your money will be devoured by builders, architects, carpenters, painters, and plumbers as if by a swarm of locusts. This trend is abetted by HGTV, the new gateway drug of the middle class.

Your authors have often wondered about the rationale behind stainless-steel appliances. We never noticed that stains on refrigerators or dishwashers were a national problem. It seemed like a quick wipe with a sponge took care of most of them. We have the same puzzlement about countertops. Most will not receive such heavy use that it is essential to carve them out of granite slabs excavated from the same quarry the Romans used to build the Pantheon. Unlike nuclear waste disposal sites, the average kitchen need not be designed to endure thousands of years.

Most kitchen countertops will not receive such heavy use that it is essential to carve them out of granite slabs excavated from the same quarry the Romans used to build the Pantheon.

DO rent rather than buy your vacation home, unless you plan to rent it out.

Unless you have lots of surplus capital and are in love with a particular place that you want to return to often for long periods, the economics will generally pencil out in favor of renting. A hotel room is a form of short-term rental that lets you preserve a lot of other options for your money.

P.S.: You will not be able to rent out your vacation home. By the time the unscrupulous management company has extracted its fees, and you have paid the maids and accounted for the thievery and scratched floors and stained sofas and broken appliances and paid yourself for the hours you spend on the phone dealing with every crisis du jour, it will not turn out to be the great investment the Realtor described. Meanwhile, all the renters clamoring to get in when you bought the property will have found a new and more exciting locale just up the road, leaving yours to sit empty month after month while your bills come due like clockwork.

DO be realistic about price when selling your home.

The classic gambit is for a Realtor to tell you that your home is worth zillions in order to get your listing, and then come back in a month and tell you that you have to slice the price drastically since—surprise!—there is no interest at that price. There is, however, an element of truth to this process. The price of your home is set by the market, period. You may have paid $10 million for your pad in Malibu during the bubble, and then spent another two million fixing it up, but that does not mean the house is now worth a $12 million. If your TV series is canceled and you can't afford the mortgage, your house is worth only what buyers will pay for it today. That might be $6 million. Realtors do not set house prices; the market does. A house has no intrinsic monetary value apart from what someone is willing to pay to rent or own it.

DON'T trade in and out of houses frequently.

Unless you are a Realtor yourself, you don't want to change homes very often. Despite the inroads made by the Internet in democratizing the real estate marketplace, transaction costs are high. A seller can spend 6 percent on commissions to a Realtor. Then there will be the costs of fixing up the house for the sale, and the months it sits on the market waiting to find a buyer. If you're a buyer, you will have inspections, fees, and closing costs on the mortgage. All in all, transaction costs in buying a home can verge on 10 percent if you are selling your old house at the same time. By comparison, you can sell a million dollars' worth of stock for $8 in one second with one mouse click.

The people we know who have made money in residential real estate are people who bought their homes 25 years ago and woke up one day to realize they were rich.

Do's and Don'ts

- Do buy a home once you are ready to settle down.

- Don't buy into a red-hot real estate market.

- Don't buy so much home that you become "house poor."

- Don't use anything but a 30-year fixed-rate mortgage unless it is a 15-year fixed-rate mortgage.

- Do let movie stars own vacation homes; you are just visiting.

- Do be realistic about how much your house is worth when selling.

- Don't move frequently. Three moves equals one fire, as the proverb says.

Chapter Twelve

Can You Still Retire Comfortably?

*Retirement Was
Overrated, Anyway*

⁓

IMAGINE THAT YOU SWITCHED on CNN to learn that a terrible Katrina-like hurricane was about to hit your city. Obviously, you would take every measure imaginable to make sure that you and your family would be safe and dry and out of harm's way.

We are here to deliver exactly such a warning. It is not a hurricane, but it is an event of such devastation that you had better keep a weather eye on it just the same. We are talking about the coming of old age. Chances are you are financially underprepared.

We have 77 million Baby Boomers rushing toward retirement. Few of them have made meaningful provision for it. About 25 percent have pension plans that should help. A few percent are millionaires. In the middle, there is a terrifying drought. The average financial savings of the Baby Boomers are far less than $50,000 per family, not counting what little equity remains in their houses. Roughly 40 percent have no savings at all.

Social Security is not a large amount for most people. Moreover, its future is uncertain. The nation is tapped out, deficitwise. The government cannot just write a check to make everything all right. That check would have to come from an ever-smaller pool of workers relative to the number of retirees. By creating massive entitlements designed to eliminate certain risks at the individual level, the government has paradoxically created gigantic new risks at a system-wide level.

Meanwhile, we face the risk of far higher inflation in the future as the dollar drifts and lurches ever lower. That means that if we have enough to retire on at age 65, by the time we reach 80, prices might have doubled. The sums that were enough at 65 will not be then. If we barely have enough to live on now, how are we going to fare when prices are twice as high?

Then there is the little matter of medical costs, which show no sign of falling. According to Kent Smetters, Wharton School professor and economist for the Congressional Budget Office, the present value of the combined shortfalls of Social Security and Medicare is between 80 and 120 trillion dollars. By comparison, the value of everything in the United States (stocks, bonds, houses, cars, toasters, etc.) is closer to $50 trillion.

This is not a problem for two groups of people: the poor and the very rich. The poor will suffer no great fall in their standard of living, because it wasn't very high in the first place. They will just migrate from one government assistance program to the next. Meanwhile, the very rich should have enough to buy the level of goods and services they need for a carefree retirement, although the government will not make it easy. Faced with gaping shortfalls and many baby (boomer) robins wanting a worm, the government will use confiscatory tax policies to shake anyone with assets upside down by the ankles for whatever coins he has. Unfortunately, this will not just hurt the very rich, but will also clean the lint from the pockets of the upper middle class as well. By *upper middle class*, we mean *you*, dear reader.

Who is going to help you when you are too old to work and your health is poor? The answer, as Roman orators from Cicero to financial wizard Ray Lucia have seen (from *De Senectute* to *Buckets of Money*), is that our younger self has to take care of our older self by putting aside sufficient savings against the ravages of age. We have to match our future assets with our future liabilities.

As Roman orators from Cicero to financial wizard Ray Lucia have seen, our younger self has to take care of our older self by putting aside sufficient savings against the ravages of age.

As when the oxygen mask falls in an airplane, you'd better start by saving yourself. Then you can start worrying about the people around you. You have good friends, even family members, who are picnicking right now, but who, a few years after retirement, will be packed off to the poor house. You may find yourself crossing the street to avoid them. The world of Boomers is going to sort itself into the fortunate few who have adequate savings and the many who do not.

Have you been to the DMV lately? The post office? It is a sobering experience. This is exactly how we will be treated at the government-run old-folks' home of the future unless we take countermeasures.

In July 2008, the accounting firm of Ernst & Young published a grim study titled, "Retirement Vulnerability of New Retirees: The Likelihood of Outliving Their Assets." You need the courage of a Cicero to read it. Looking at the prospects for middle-class Americans nearing retirement who don't have defined-benefit pension plans, they conclude that on average we would immediately need to cut our standard of living by 42 percent to have a shot at not going broke when we are old. If we fail to take this step, our odds of running out of money rise to 79 percent. Cutting back 42 percent is more than dropping HBO and lattes. It's more like cutting off an arm and a leg.

These numbers are the death knell for the middle-class dream of retiring to a life slicing Titleists and country club cocktailing. Notice that this report was assembled before the stock market panic clipped another 30 percent from the Dow and home prices "corrected" to the downside. Now even Ernst & Young's predictions look optimistic.

Calculating Your Somewhat-Safe Withdrawal Rate

Retirees want to know what the safe withdrawal rate from their nest egg is. This would be the percentage of assets that they can draw from their portfolios during year one of retirement, and then continue to withdraw every year thereafter for the rest of their lives, adjusting the amount by inflation over time.

There is no such thing as a safe withdrawal rate. The safe withdrawal rate is *zero*. The best we can do is estimate a somewhat-safe withdrawal rate.

～

There is no such thing as a safe withdrawal rate. The safe withdrawal rate is *zero*.

Here's a simple way of looking at the problem: If we plan for a 10 percent chance of running out of money, and a 10 percent chance of living to age 100, we end up with a 1 percent chance (10% × 10%) of arriving at age 100 and having no money. This seems like a reasonable risk level, but all such calculations are just educated guesses. If you want a guarantee, buy a toaster.

Some retirement gurus think that the smart way to plan your retirement is to save money until the day you retire, and then either put it all into an immediate annuity or into Treasury inflation-protected bonds and then live off the interest. These strategies are problematic. As we have seen, the immediate annuity requires an act of faith in the insurance company and the government's calculation of the Consumer Price Index (CPI), which may or may not represent inflation as you experience it. The TIPs solution also depends on the CPI, and assumes that you can live on 2 percent of your savings. That would leave most of us dining on soda crackers.

The alternative is to live off our investment portfolios, with the likelihood of gradually drawing down principal over time. Table 12.1 indicates our current estimates of how much we can draw annually from the various Tangent Portfolios under these assumptions.

To begin, find your age on the left-hand column. Round your age down: If you are 63, use age 60. If you are married, use the age of the younger spouse. Then, go to the next column to find the maximum percent of your nest egg you can withdraw, depending on the annual risk of loss you are willing to take.

Every year thereafter, until you reach your next five-year milestone, withdraw the same dollar amount you took the first year, adjusted for inflation. The government has a handy online calculator (http://data.bls.gov/cgi-bin/cpicalc.pl) where you can punch in the dollar amount you pulled out the first year and it will adjust it for inflation to the

Table 12.1   Tangent Portfolio Somewhat-Safe Withdrawal Rates

Age	Tangent 20	Tangent 25	Tangent 33
60	3.1%	3.3%	3.5%
65	3.3%	3.6%	3.6%
70	3.8%	3.9%	4.0%
75	4.2%	4.3%	4.4%
80	4.9%	5.0%	5.1%
85	6.1%	6.1%	6.1%
90	8.6%	8.6%	8.5%

current year, thus calculating your current withdrawal amount in one easy step. Don't say Uncle Sam never gave you nothing.

At your next five-year milestone, go across the chart to the safe withdrawal percentage corresponding to your age, and start the process over. Multiply this higher percentage times the present value of your nest egg to arrive at the new amount you can withdraw. Note that this might be more or less money than the year before, depending on how your portfolio has performed in the interim. Your income in retirement will fluctuate, just as it probably did before you retired. For the next four years, adjust this new dollar amount by inflation and make your withdrawals. Then, after another five years have passed, move down the table to the next withdrawal rate, and so on.

This method, originally proposed by your authors, has subsequently found confirmation in the academic literature by John Spitzer, Emeritus Professor of Economics at SUNY. Keep in mind that the sustainable withdrawal rates in Table 12.1 are exclusively for use with the Tangent Portfolios. They are net of fund expenses but gross of management fees, if any. They are not set in stone and may change over time. If you are a do-it-yourselfer, and even if you are not, we recommend using quant savant Geoff

Table 12.2 Estimated Estates

Age	Tangent 20	Tangent 25	Tangent 33
Estate at Average Life Expectancy	$760,681	$955,059	$1,135,703

Considine's QPP Portfolio Planner (www.quantext.com) to calculate your withdrawal rates on an ongoing basis.

A tradeoff with the withdrawal rate is the resulting size of your estate. The more you withdraw along the way, the smaller your final estate will be. Withdrawal rates are estimated with an eye toward lowering your risk of running out of money at the extremes of old age and poor market returns. To determine your likely estate size, we can make assumptions that are more forgiving, using median investment returns and an average lifespan. Table 12.2 assumes you retired at age 65 with $500,000 in your nest egg and took withdrawals as in Table 12.1. As before, the results are net of fund expenses but do not include any management fees.

While you cannot take this to the bank, it does give you a back-of-the-envelope calculation of the size of your estate (at least, for your liquid financial assets) under these assumptions and shows the tradeoff between portfolio risk, your withdrawal rates, and the final estate you might pass on to your heirs.

When You Care Enough to Give Yourself the Very Best

If you are retired and can't make ends meet, you have several options, which you can use singly or in combination. The best choice is to *unretire* by rejoining the labor force. Any income stream you can generate will stretch your nest egg like Silly Putty.

From there the choices get harder. You can relocate to a place where the cost of living is lower than it is where you live now. Cities and states vary tremendously in their cost of living, and you can find one you like at Sperling's Best Places (www.bestplaces.net). If you are willing to retire to Mexico or Belize or Costa Rica, your dollar will go even further. This is a drastic step, but you will have plenty of company. It beats staying home and going broke.

An Immediate Annuity

Taking it to the next level, you can cash in whatever savings are left and put them into an annuity.

When you buy an immediate annuity, you hand an insurance company a sum of money and they parcel it back to you a little at a time, over the rest of your life, no matter how long you may live. The older you are when you buy an annuity, the more it will pay you, because the shorter your remaining estimated lifespan will be.

Naturally, there are downsides:

- Your principal is gone.
- You will need an inflation-adjusted policy, which pays out less in order to compensate for the risk of inflation.
- While the income from an annuity is guaranteed, who guarantees the guarantee? The money belongs to the insurer. They may have been run prudently for 200 years, but all it takes is one whiz kid with an MBA to ruin it. States do offer guarantees but read the fine print. Circumstances where the insurance companies go bust are not going to be times when the state coffers are exactly overflowing with revenue, either.

An ad from the January 1946 issue of *Life* magazine features Phoenix Mutual's Retirement Income Plan, an annuity that promises to Guarantee Your Future. It shows a still-vibrant elderly couple walking along the beach (why are seniors always portrayed walking on the beach? Is this a polite way of reminding them that they are on the cusp of eternity?). The caption reads: "It's fun to grow old when you have no money worries." The text goes on to promise an income of $100 a month starting at age 55. This date of the ad is especially telling, because if you had bought that annuity in April 1946, by April 1947 you would be 56 years old and that mouth-watering $100-a-month income for life would spend like only $82.78 thanks to inflation, and you still have another 30 or 40 years to go. Before long, you wouldn't just be walking on the beach, you'd be sleeping there, too.

Why are seniors always portrayed walking on the beach? Is this a polite way of reminding them that they are on the cusp of eternity?

The Last Resort

Your last recourse is to take out a *reverse mortgage*: A bank will let you use your residence as a piggy bank and will send you a monthly check against its value, with the amount actuarially adjusted over the rest of your life. What's more, they cannot kick you out unless you fail to maintain the property (paying your taxes, making repairs, maintaining insurance). Even if you end up pulling out more than the value of your home, the lender cannot attach any other assets beyond the house itself.

It sounds like a crackerjack deal, but it may not hold the prize you expect:

- Fees are steep and paid up front.
- Government-backed reverse mortgage loans have low dollar payouts.

- Private reverse mortgages have higher payouts but also higher fees.
- Once you move out of your residence (for example, if you have to go to a nursing home) the bank can seize it. Your home needs to be set up for elder care.
- Your monthly check will be eroded by inflation.
- What if your neighborhood goes downhill, or your children move to another state?

For all of these reasons, a reverse mortgage is a last resort. Break glass only after you have exhausted all other possibilities. If you want to explore this option further, the AARP has a handy pamphlet titled, "Reverse Mortgage Loans: Borrowing Against Your Home" that will be your starting point.

Retirement Planning Do's and Don'ts

DON'T retire.

The best option of all is never to retire. In fact, we need to retire the whole idea of retirement. Hang onto your job as long as you can.

We need to retire the whole idea of retirement.

Writing in the *Financial Analysts Journal*, Robert Arnott and Anne Casscells estimate that the retirement age will have to rise to 72 or 73 by the year 2030 to keep the same ratio of younger workers supporting older retirees that we have today. This will happen almost automatically, as people see they don't have enough assets to retire and so keep working longer. With a relative shortage of younger people to take their place, companies might be willing to keep older workers on the payroll, especially if the high insurance costs of older employees can be offloaded to the government (which is to say, everyone else).

If you have a job where you will be forced to retire, then set up a second career you can launch when (or preferably before) you leave your current one. The longer you can keep a paycheck coming in, the happier you will be. For every extra year we work, our nest eggs have one more year to grow and one fewer year to support us. This compression works in your favor.

DO replenish your savings.

Periodically we read an investing column in a newspaper or magazine about how to save our 401(k) plan after the damage of 2008. This invariably occasions a bitter, mirthless chortle in your authors' esophaguses. There is no magic way to save your 401(k) except by putting in lots more new, freshly earned money.

The most obvious answer is to save more. This works best if you are in your twenties and can somehow squirrel away enough to let the compound interest provide for your retirement. However, for most of us, the bright elusive butterfly of youth has flown. This means cinching our belts and forgoing present consumption in the service of long-term goals—exactly what we Boomers have specialized in avoiding all our lives.

DON'T take Social Security right away.

Should you apply for Social Security benefits as soon as possible (age 62), or as late as possible (age 70)? There are two schools of thought here and they lead to opposite courses of action. Let us confuse you:

- **The argument for applying early:** Social Security will probably be means-tested and as a middle-class person you won't qualify for much, if anything, in the way of benefits, so grab a few bucks from the system before they slam the door. This same argument applies if you do not have longevity in your family history, since you may not live long enough to collect what you could.

- **The argument for applying late:** The value of the inflation-adjusted annuity promised by Social Security is disproportionately high, so you should postpone taking it until the last possible moment. This makes sense if you are longlived and/or if you believe that Social Security will continue to pay out something like its present level of benefits to a person of your economic status.

Other things equal, we prefer to wait until age 70, since the government is paying you 8 percent a year to defer taking your benefits until then. That's a good deal, if it comes true. It also should increase your spouse's benefit if he or she outlives you.

DON'T take a lump-sum payout from your pension plan without doing your homework.

Usually, when they are eager to provide you with a lump sum payout it is because they have determined that it is a good deal for them. It may not be such a good deal for you. It is simple to check: Just find out what the amount they are going to pay you would be worth if you immediately reinvested it into an immediate annuity. If you can get more just by turning around and reinvesting it yourself, then take it. You also might want to take it if you fear your company's plan is on the brink of insolvency.

Do's and Don'ts

- Do postpone retirement as long as possible. The safest time to retire is *never*.

- Do relocate to an area with a lower cost of living to have a higher standard of living.

- Do use an immediate, inflation-adjusted annuity to convert your nest egg into the maximum amount of income, but the longer you can put off buying it and the higher interest rates are at the time, the higher the payout you should receive.

- Don't take out a reverse mortgage except as a last resort.

- Do recalculate your withdrawal rate every five years during retirement. You may be able to increase your payout.

- Do replenish your savings as aggressively as you can.

- Don't take Social Security as soon as you are eligible. It often pays to delay.

- Don't blindly accept a lump-sum payout from your pension plan.

Chapter Thirteen

The End Game

~

"If Something Cannot Go on Forever, It Will Stop"

AT SOME POINT, we will all have to pack our bags and enter immortality. There are some definite do's and don'ts to leaving things in good order for those you love and are leaving behind.

We know what you're thinking: *Who cares if I leave a huge mess? Not my problem!* Okay, but consider this:

---

*The quote at the chapter opener is in the words of Ben's father, the noted economist, Herbert Stein.

You're lying immobilized on a table. All it would take is some simple medical procedure to revive you. Meanwhile, an unscrupulous doctor is thinking, "That liver. Those kidneys. I could get rich selling them on the black market. It would be wrong, of course. Still, that new Porsche looks awfully tasty. . . ." Well, without giving a trusted person a durable medical power of attorney, who will stop him from harvesting your organs for his bank account?

A Will and a Way

Do have a will. Contrary to popular superstition, not having a will does not prevent you from dying. While this might seem like a clever way to trick God into letting you live forever, He sees through the gambit and is not deterred from sending His coachman at the appointed hour. True, not everyone needs a will. If you are a derelict living on the streets with no possessions and no known relations, there is no need to call your attorney for an appointment.

Otherwise, if you have a pulse, you need to do some estate planning. Get a referral to an attorney who specializes in this area from one of your friends who is more responsible than you are. That lawyer who fixed your traffic ticket is probably not the right guy. If your life situation is simple and straightforward, you might even be able to prepare a will online at www.legalzoom.com.

~

**If you have a pulse, you need to do some
estate planning. Get a referral to an attorney.
That lawyer who fixed your traffic ticket is
probably not the right guy.**

Without a will, you die intestate. This should not be
confused with dying on the interstate (although that may
happen as well if you drink and drive). It means that state
law will determine how your assets are distributed. This
process is run by the probate court and is slow, completely
public, and expensive.

Here's what you need:

- A **Will**, where you will name someone to manage
  your estate and say how your property will be transferred at death. If you already have a will, but it was
  drafted during the Truman administration, it may
  be time to freshen it up a bit.
- A **Revocable Trust,** which will hold your assets. It
  will be administered by a trustee whom you will appoint
  on behalf of beneficiaries whom you will name.

  There are lots of other cool trusts that you
  might need depending on the size and complexity
  of your estate and your particular life situation.
  This is not the sort of thing you can just do by

downloading a form from the Internet. You need to talk to an attorney.

- A **Durable Power of Attorney for Health Care**, naming someone to make medical decisions on your behalf in the event that you cannot communicate.

- Possibly, a **Durable Power of Attorney for Finances**, so someone can look after your money in your (mental) absence.

- A **Living Will**, directing anyone as to what kind of heroic measures you want medical personnel to take to extend your life if you are not able to make your wishes known.

"We're Spending Our Kids' Inheritances"

"We're Spending Our Kids' Inheritances" is a great bumpersticker. However, are you spending them in the right order?

The conventional wisdom is that you should spend down taxable accounts first, and only later pull money out of IRAs. This lets the assets compound inside the IRA wrapper without being taxed along the way. It defers any taxes you might owe, since your IRA withdrawals would be taxed at ordinary income rates. Is this a good idea?

Not always. When you join the choir invisible, your heirs will receive a step-up in the cost basis on the assets in your taxable accounts. Although they may have to pay estate taxes to get them, they would receive these taxable assets with a new cost basis that in one stroke wipes out your lifetime of embedded capital gains taxes.

The (non-Roth) IRAs your children inherit will have them singing a different tune. They will have to pay taxes at their marginal rates on the distributions, less a credit for estate taxes already paid. Depending on circumstances, your children might be better off if you were to draw down your retirement accounts first and leave the taxable accounts in your estate—the opposite of what is usually counseled. If you think you might fall into this category, give your accountant a jingle. Or Mr. Obama. All this depends on the estate and marginal tax rate schedules of the future, a total unknown. The government can and will change the rules.

The Joy of Illiquid Assets

While we're tossing out gratuitous tax advice, let's share another thought. When it comes time to value your estate for tax purposes, if you hold liquid financial assets like stocks and bonds and mutual funds, it is going to be extremely easy to come up with the correct amount of estate tax to pay. All the IRS has to do is look in the paper on the day you die or the day six months later and pick whichever set of prices gives your estate the lowest value. (Because nothing is ever simple with the IRS, you have to use the average price of the stock throughout the day, not the closing price.) Anyone using this method can value your financial assets to the penny, and there is no disputing those valuations.

Now imagine that you have a large estate. To the extent that you own nonfinancial assets, the valuation process is going to become more open to interpretation. If you own art, or oriental rugs, or houses, or a boat, or vintage automobiles, you may end up paying less in the way of estate tax on these items. That is because these types of assets forgo a liquidity premium. You cannot readily turn them into cash the way you can a stock or a mutual fund. Selling them is laborious and may take months. There may not be another oriental rug exactly like yours so the pricing is going to be a matter of judgment. Your estate will have to hire an appraiser, and if the IRS doesn't like the valuation, then it's going to be appraiser versus appraiser. There is a lot more room for negotiation here than when discussing what Fidelity Contrafund sold for at the close on June 23. Illiquid assets are difficult to value precisely and where the valuation can be expressed along a range, you can claim the conservative end of that range. Consequently, you may be able to save on your estate tax. The tradeoff is that many of these illiquid assets many not be great investments in and of themselves. You make the call.

Get Organized

When you die, the people around you are going to be crazed with grief. At exactly this point, they will also have to go through all your vital papers in order to bury you and then keep the wolf from the door. There will be no shortage of "helpers" descending on them at this vulnerable point. You will be doing your family a great service if you prepare a document outlining where everything is and how to get at it. It will inject a note of sanity to an otherwise insane time.

Here is what they will need:

- Your wishes for your funeral, noting any arrangements you have already made. If you are considerate enough to set this up prior to checkout time, it can cost your family far less than when they are grief-stricken and ready to sign any piece of paper the unctuous undertaker puts in front of them.
- Contact information for your priest, minister, or rabbi.
- The name and contact information for your estate attorney, accountant, insurance agent, broker, and investment advisor.
- Access information for your various online accounts like e-mail, personal websites, and any social

networking sites you might use such as Facebook, MySpace, or LinkedIn.

- The location of your past three years' income tax returns.
- A list of every investment account you own (bank accounts, CDs, brokerage accounts, IRAs, hedge funds, annuities, etc.) along with the account numbers, account registrations, custodians, online access URLs, user IDs, and the location of the most recent statements. Find some other way to give them the passwords lest this document fall into enemy hands.
- The beneficiaries of your retirement accounts.
- Notes about any software (Quicken, Money, Quickbooks, Excel spreadsheets, etc.) you use to track your finances.
- A list of all property you own (including automobiles), how each is titled, where the title papers are, as well as the relevant information about the mortgages and loans against them.
- A list of any special debts that you may owe, beyond those already covered.
- Survivors will be especially interested in any life insurance policies you might own, which they will hope you paid for with after-tax dollars and are held in an irrevocable life insurance trust (ILIT) so the proceeds will not be taxed as part of your estate.

- Your wishes regarding the disposition of any special possessions. This may not be legally binding but it might be useful to your executor.
- Anything you think somebody ought to know about your situation that is not already covered above.

As wonderful as it is to have all this written down, it won't do your executors much good unless they are actually able to lay their hands on this master document. Make sure they have a copy or will find it within one minute of casual looking through your desk.

You are not doing your spouse any favors by sparing her (or him) from the headaches of understanding your family finances. She should have a general idea of what you own, what you owe, what is involved in dealing with it from month to month, and especially whom you would trust to help her with it in your absence.

Do's and Don'ts for Your Financial Legacy

Here are some ideas in case you are still lucky enough to have a few coins burning a hole in your pocket or just want to do good onto others:

DO write love letters.

Now is as good a time as any to let those close to you know how much you have always loved and appreciated them. You might assume they already know, but why not take five minutes and tell them so they do not have to use a Ouija board to find out. It might be the most important letter they ever receive, and it might even do you some good to write it, too. You can always leave these in your personal files to be discovered later if you don't want to deal with any mawkish responses.

DO pay to educate junior.

If you are staring at a big potential estate tax, one thing you will want to do is to make sure that your heirs are well-educated. You can do this by opening a West Virginia 529 Plan for every child and grandchild. The West Virginia plan gives you access to the coveted Dimensional Funds at reasonable expense. You and your spouse can each contribute $13,000 per year exempt from gift tax, and you can make the first five years' contributions in year one (for a total of $130,000 if both you and your spouse contribute). Put the money in the appropriate age-based portfolio and forget it. After it seasons for a couple of years, that money should be protected from creditors and removed from your estate.

Are you concerned that your children or grandchildren may not require further education? If the money is not used for college tuition, any earnings will be subject to income tax and a 10 percent penalty upon withdrawal. Still, not a bad price for possibly decades of tax-free compounding.

DO pay for your grandchildren's retirement.

Here is an excellent use of a variable annuity. As soon as the little munchkins are born and stamped with a Social Security number, open a variable annuity for them. You and your spouse can each contribute $13,000 a year tax free as a gift (though not if you've also given them $13,000 that same year to a 529 plan, as above). The annuity will have to be placed inside a UTMA/UGMA account, which Vanguard (www.vanguard.com) is happy to do. Put half the money into the Total U.S. Stock Market and half into the Total International Stock Market. As these amounts compound over the next 70 years tax free, your grandchildren might find that there's enough money here to pay for their entire retirement. That's the power of compound interest and saving early.

Once the grandchildren are no longer minors, they will have the power to pry open the annuities and take the money out for any nefarious purpose they want. If they turn out to be crack addicts, they won't care about the penalties, just whatever cash they can get their hands on. This is a risk. If they are good kids and leave it alone, it has the power to do them a world of good in later life.

DO be charitable.

If you are fortunate enough to be able to leave money to charities, you can vet them online to make sure the executives are not spending your money flying to Bali on private jets. Two good watchdogs are Charity Navigator (www .charitynavigator.org) and the American Institute of Philanthropy (www.charitywatch.org). It is always a good idea to make sure your dollars are used efficiently for the actual cause whose name appears on the letterhead.

Unless you have tens of millions of dollars to give away, there is little argument for starting a family charitable foundation any more. Schwab, Fidelity, and Vanguard all offer charitable funds that will take your money today, invest it in low-expense index funds, and distribute it on any timetable and to any charitable organizations that you (or your heirs) desire. They take care of all the legal and administrative work for a fraction of what you would pay to replicate these services on your own. You can go online and make gifts to charity whenever you want. Why use custom-tailoring when an off-the-rack model costs a fraction as much and works better?

Unless you have tens of millions of dollars to give away, there is little argument for starting a family charitable foundation these days.

One excellent feature of these donor-advised funds is that they allow you to make tax-deductible donations during your high-income years, and then distribute the money after you have retired and no longer need the tax break.

DO be a yield hound.

Some seniors enjoy the hobby of constantly moving their cash to wherever they can get insured deposits at the highest rates. These folks are the nemesis of banks, who advertise "teaser" rates to build their balance sheets and then lower them once the cash is in the vault and the account holder has gone to sleep. Websites like www. checkingfinder.com can help you locate who has the hot deals right now.

For this to work, you have to stay on top of the yields and be willing to move your money at the drop of a basis point. If you are not going to put in this extra effort, a money market fund at Vanguard will typically have the highest non-trick yield.

Seniors with millions in cash to park sometimes worry about where they can get FDIC insurance on cash balances running into the millions of dollars, when each account is insured by the government to merely $100,000 or $250,000 at most. A local bank participating in the CDARS program (www.cdars.com) will farm up to

$50,000,000 out to a number of certificates of deposit at banks all over the country, each one of which will be insured, and rolled over when needed, and with the reporting consolidated onto one convenient statement. While there are many participating banks, the Bank of New York Mellon administers the program and might give you a slightly higher rate if you start there (www .bnymellon.com).

CDs at credit unions often offer even higher rates than those offered by banks. These are also insured by the government (the NCUA versus the FDIC), which undercharges them for the insurance it provides, meaning that U.S. taxpayers effectively subsidize your yield. There is more work involved in finding a credit union with the highest rate on CDs, and then to join it, but a truly motivated yield hound can usually find a way. As we said, it's a hobby.

Do's and Don'ts

- Do have a will, plus all the other legal apparatus you need in order to depart this vale of tears with things in good order for those you leave behind.

- Do consider tax-saving estate giving strategies, such as 529 plans and annuities, for your grandchildren if you can afford it.

- Do leave a detailed list telling your survivors the *who, what, where, when,* and *how* of your financial empire.

- Don't start a family foundation unless you are as rich as Bill Gates.

- Do get the highest yield you can on your cash balances.

So Long, Farewell

───────── ∾ ─────────

WE HOPE THAT YOU WILL PROFIT from these meditations on bulletproofing your investments, both personal and financial.

In closing, here are a few thoughts on our collective financial predicament.

Our generation is coming into the home stretch with less in the way of financial resources than we anticipated, and certainly much less than we would have wished for. However, this is not the end of the world. The hamster wheel we are on can never get us ahead of our wants, but it can get us well ahead of what we need.

We may retire to a small town instead of a country club. We may have to play golf at a public course. We may drive a Camry instead of a Cadillac. We may travel to our national parks and not to Bora Bora. These might be disappointments, but they are scarcely privations. We might even be better off for them.

There will be a college nearby, where we can expand our minds. There will be a public library, with more great books than we will be able to read in our lifetimes, allowing us to spend our retirement consulting the greatest thinkers who ever lived. Every piece of music ever recorded will be digitally available at our fingertips, and every film ever made waiting for our DVD players. There will be first-class sporting events and quality entertainment on television, and the Internet putting us in touch with a global village almost for free, and computers extending our powers to create, calculate, and communicate in ways unavailable even a generation ago. There will be long walks down leafy lanes. There will be time to contemplate the beauties of nature, for art and photography, for poetry and philosophy. There will be time for friends and family, and time for meditation and solitude.

Do take advantage of these opportunities.

This will also be your chance to volunteer, to give something back, to do something to help those less fortunate than yourself. If not now, when?

It's like the old joke: A man dies and finally gets to the gates of Heaven. He tells St. Peter, "God has a lot to answer for. There's all this suffering and injustice in the world. Why didn't he do anything about it?"

To which St. Peter replies, "What a coincidence! I was just going to ask you the same thing."

Acknowledgments

———————— ∼ ————————

BEN STEIN WISHES TO THANK the editors of the *Wall Street Journal*, *Barron's*, the *New York Times*, *Yahoo! Finance*, *Fortune* magazine, and especially the *American Spectator* for allowing him to write about these subjects for many years.

Both authors wish to thank their agents, Lois Wallace (Ben) and Bob Diforio (Phil), as well as the whole gang at John Wiley & Sons—especially Debra Englander and Kelly O'Connor, who made producing this book such a pleasure.

About the Authors

~

BEN STEIN can be seen talking about finance on Fox TV news every week and writes about it regularly in *Fortune* magazine and the *American Spectator*. Not only is he the son of the world-famous economist and government advisor Herbert Stein, but Ben is a respected economist in his own right. He received his BA with honors in economics from Columbia University in 1966, studied economics in the graduate school of economics at Yale while he earned his law degree there, and worked as an economist for the Department of Commerce. He taught law and economics for many years at Pepperdine Law School.

Ben Stein is known to many as a movie and television personality, especially from *Ferris Bueller's Day Off* and from his long-running quiz show, *Win Ben Stein's Money*. But he has probably worked more in personal and corporate finance than anything else. He has written about finance for *Barron's* and the *Wall Street Journal* for decades, and was a columnist for the *New York Times* for many years. He was one of the chief busters of the junk-bond frauds of the 1980s, has been a longtime critic of corporate executives' self-dealing, and has co-written eight self-help books about personal finance. He frequently travels the country speaking about finance in both serious and humorous ways, and is a regular contributor to *CBS Sunday Morning*, Fox News Network, and CNN.

Website: www.benstein.com

PHIL DEMUTH was the valedictorian of his class at the University of California at Santa Barbara in 1972, and then took his master's in communications and PhD in clinical psychology. Both a psychologist and an investment advisor, Phil has written for the *Wall Street Journal*, *Barron's*, the *Journal of Financial Planning*, and *forbes.com*, as well as *Human Behavior* and *Psychology Today*, and is co-author of seven books with Ben Stein. His opinions have been quoted in *theStreet.com*, *Yahoo! Finance*, *On Wall Street*, and *Fortune* magazine, and he has been profiled in

Research magazine and seen on *Forbes on Fox*, *Wall Street Week*, and various CNBC shows. As if all this were not enough, Phil also served as a judge on *America's Most Smartest Model*. He is managing director of Conservative Wealth Management LLC in Los Angeles, and a registered investment advisor to high-net-worth individuals, institutions, and foundations.

Website: www.phildemuth.com.